An Unexpected Journal

The Merits & Myths of Modernity

Spring 2024
Volume 7, Issue 1

Copyright © 2024 An Unexpected Journal

Print Edition

Credits

Editor-in-Chief: Jasmin Biggs
President: Annie Nardone
Issue Editors: Jasmin Biggs, Jim Swayze
Cover Image: Grant Broadhurst
Journal Mark: Erika McMillan
Journal Design and Layout: Legacy Marketing Services
Editors: Jasmin Biggs, Grant Broadhurst, Annie Crawford, Karise Gililland, Annie Nardone, Megan Prahl, Zak Schmoll
Contributors: Jasmin Biggs, Suzanne Carol, Annie Crawford, Karise Gililland, Sarah Hadley, Seth Myers, Annie Nardone, Josiah Peterson, Thomas Sims, Megan M. Starr, Jason M. Smith, James M. Swayze, Joshua Jo Wah Yen

All rights reserved. This book is protected by the copyright laws of the United States of America. No part of this publication may be reproduced, distributed or transmitted in any form or by any means, or stored in a database or retrieval system, without prior written permission.

An Unexpected Journal
Houston, TX

https://www.anunexpectedjournal.com
Email: anunexpectedjournal@gmail.com

&

Wootton Major Publishing
Austin, TX

https://www.woottonmajorpublishing.com

Contents

Introduction v
    Jasmin Biggs

Why Christians Should Embrace Progress (Rightly Defined) 1
    Jasmin Biggs

Review: *Many Times and Many Places* **by K. Alan Snyder and Jamin Metcalf** 10
    Josiah Peterson

From Medieval to Modern and Beyond 15
    Seth Myers

To Live Dangerously or Die Trying 41
    Sarah Hadley

The Groundwork of Secularism: The Gifts of Modernity 47
    Joshua Jo Wah Yen

Modern Art–Is It That Awful? 65
    Annie Nardone

Hamlet and the Headless World 74
    Annie Crawford

After the Light 83
    James M. Swayze

Freeing Michelangelo's Prisoners 86
    By Jasmin Biggs

Pink Faux Fur 100
    Suzanne Carol

Bent Binding 104
    Thomas Sims

Reckoning with Death and Dying in a Disenchanted Age: The Christian Reality of the Fear of Death 106
    Megan M. Starr

***Quiddity*: A Dizain** 122
    Karise Gililland

Pious Transaction or Blessed Exploit? Theologies of Nature from Paganism to Modernity 126
    Jason Smith

the spirit of intellectual hospitality and brotherly love, that we may sharpen one other and our readers alike. We hope each of our perspectives will aid in broadening and deepening your understanding of a pivotal movement that fundamentally shapes our daily lives. May you find our humble words illuminating and edifying.

Gratia et veritas,

Jasmin Biggs
Editor-in-Chief

Why Christians Should Embrace Progress (Rightly Defined)

Jasmin Biggs

Introduction

Chronological snobbery is an iconic phrase dubbed by C.S. Lewis to describe prejudice against an era. In his memoir *Surprised by Joy*, he recalls exclaiming, "Why—damn it—it's medieval," continuing, "I still had all the chronological snobbery of my period and used the names of the earlier periods as terms of abuse."[1] It was common for his community to denigrate the past. But I was raised in a branch of conservative evangelicalism that practiced chronological snobbery in the opposite direction: the term "modern" was often used as a term of derision. Concepts like "cultural," "modernity," and "progress" were often bashed, and in their place, we sought to recreate some wholesome, by-gone era through the supposed dress code, social norms, and lifestyle of prior generations.[2] In essence, to partake of modern culture and lifestyle was to be (at best) theologically compromised, communally fragmented, technologically addicted, and morally unclean. And to be sure, there are many fair and urgent critiques to be made of modern life and thought. But Christians today can inadvertently fall into another form of chronological snobbery when we carry a subconscious or

---

1 C. S. Lewis, *Surprised by Joy* (New York: HarperCollins, 2017), 206-208.
2 For more on this, see *Shiny Happy People*, the Amazon documentary regarding the Duggar family of the hit TV show *19 Kids & Counting*. Other figureheads included Bill Gothard, Doug Phillips, Voddie Baucham, and the now-defunct Vision Forum. A popular representative of this posture today is Doug Wilson, pastor at Christ Church in Moscow, Idaho.

moderns also believe they can progress beyond their need for the Vine, clinging to the fruit of a just society while rejecting the just God who grounds natural law. If we progress beyond the foundation that makes progress possible, we will fall into the void. Clearly, progress should neither be unequivocally praised nor unilaterally condemned.

So my goal in this essay is to provide a fresh paradigm for understanding progress, that we may be equipped to evaluate both history and the modern era fairly. It will help us to appreciate both the past and the present without idolizing either. It will enable us to resist chronological snobbery in either direction, that we may discover and cherish God's natural revelation wherever he chooses to reveal it.

Horizontal vs. Vertical Progress

We might think of progress as the patron idol of secular modernity. It is the attitude that anything new is better, and anything old is obsolete. By and large, the secular world sees progress as horizontal and sequential. It's as if history were a lengthy row of dominoes proceeding down a dark corridor, with the spotlight of truth, goodness, and human flourishing resting only on the foremost dominoes. Meanwhile, the fallen dominoes disappear down the hall into a void of thick darkness. In this view, we are the heroes of history, the refined and enlightened moderns looking down our noses at the bloody, brutish barbarians of past eras. This is chronological snobbery, writ large. Yet Christians unwittingly accept this horizontal view when we wrench the spotlight onto some different set of historical dominoes and cast today's dominoes into shadow, arguing that some other era is the pinnacle of goodness, truth, and human flourishing. Both views commit the error of chronological snobbery. But there is another way to view progress that squares more truly with Scripture.

Suppose we imagine progress to be vertical and cumulative rather than horizontal and sequential. 1 Peter 2 presents the Christian Church as a temple made of 'living stones' which are "built up as a spiritual house to be a holy priesthood and to offer spiritual sacrifices that are acceptable to God through Jesus Christ."[7] The *Imago Dei* in every person means that every living stone contributes to a vertical edifice, a temple that rises ever higher, accumulating ever more knowledge and depth of insight. Jesus himself is the "chosen and precious cornerstone" of this Church.

Picture a heap of stones. Each stone on its own is not a temple. It cannot remotely pass for one, though it might like to put on airs. But when built together into a cathedral of great height, some stones will, in fact, see farther than others. After all, the view from the top is greater than the view from the base. Because of this, the stones near the top of the edifice may arrogantly presume to be more "progressed," They have, after all, a better view. But that view is due to no merit of their own. They possess no superior intellect by the sheer accident of placement. The view they enjoy is only possible because of layers upon layers of other stones that brought them up to that height. In fact, in order to truly see clearly, a stone must first understand the cumulative insights of the stones that have gone before. But stones that refuse to learn the lessons of history are just as naturally ignorant and entrenched in their cultural mud as any stone a thousand years ago. By understanding the layers of stones that have gone before, each stone will find its place in the whole structure. It may perhaps gain a clearer vision than the stones on the lower levels, but this clearer vision is due to no merit or greater brilliance of its own, but due merely to a willingness to be built up and edified by the whole structure.

We see, then, how when rightly understood, progress is cumulative and vertical. It depends not on the renunciation of everything prior to the Now, but rather on the embrace of the best of natural revelation in every era of human history. In other words, a Christian view of progress means that we do not merely react to history, like dominos forming a line.

---

[7] 1 Peter 2:5b (NET)

Rather, we build upon history, like stones forming a cathedral. (This also requires learning our true history, of which most of us are terribly illiterate.) Furthermore, in Christ are all the treasures of wisdom and knowledge.[8] So we may also delight in the treasures of natural revelation discovered by non-Christians on a variety of subjects, bringing those treasures into Christ's temple.

Again, simply being a stone near the top of the cathedral does not make it superior to stones below it. Some stones near the top are ornamental gargoyles, embellishments that lend beauty and whimsy to the cathedral's aesthetics, while some stones near the base are crucial to the cathedral's structural integrity. And some stones near the top will themselves be structural pillars for the insights and progress of the next generation.

In other words, I am not arguing that modern figures like Martin Luther King Jr., Albert Einstein, or Isaac Newton are innately more intelligent, moral, or enlightened than earlier historical figures like Thomas Aquinas, St. Augustine, or Plato. But there is a very real sense in which later figures have an advantage that earlier figures lack: the opportunity to reap the benefits of more cumulative progress. When we build upon the foundation of all the knowledge and wisdom that has accumulated through our predecessors, we can see farther.

For example, we have a better understanding of science in the year 2024 than in 1524. But we also have a worse understanding of the unity of beauty, goodness, and truth in 2024 than we did in 1524. For true progress to take place, humanity must consciously take hold of the best of every era, from ancient times to today, to build a holistic, cumulative vision.

For those still skeptical that progress is possible, it is a fact that more books exist in 2024 than in 1924, and more in 1924 than in 1024. If a "book" is "recorded data," then we have more recorded data now than ever before. Some portion of that data

---

8 Colossians 2:2-3.

turns out to be false, the dross that burns away; and some portion ultimately graduates to the category of knowledge. In that sense, knowledge accumulates. If some imaginary person in 2024 could absorb all existing knowledge *and* apply it rightly, we would think them wiser than another imaginary person in 1024 who did the same. Hence, cumulative progress is possible.

Note well that affirming the value of progress does not entail an embrace of secular progressivism *per se*. Secular progressivism adheres more closely to that horizontal view of progress discussed earlier. It depends on the renunciation of the past as largely worthless and an overinflation of ourselves as fundamentally wiser and better than our forebears. But progress, understood vertically, rightly values the best of the past *and* the best of the present. It avoids the trap of chronological snobbery in either direction.

Why We Still Need Progress

One might wonder whether we even need progress today. Some might think that since we have Scripture, human thought is unnecessary. Don't we already have everything we need in Scripture? I affirm that the biblical canon is closed and must be respected. We most certainly must hold a high view of Scripture. But a high view of any tool means using it as intended, not insisting on using that tool for tasks that the master craftsman gave us other tools for. I do not treat a sword with respect or esteem if I use it as a sledgehammer. The purpose of Scripture is to reveal the character of God, the plan of salvation through Jesus Christ, and timeless principles for right living. It is not to tell us the exact details of how to embody those principles in every situation.

So applied theology, or orthopraxy, must be developed in each era as the needs of the moment arise. Theological progress is made when we seek to creatively apply the timeless principle to the specific, embodied situation, building on the insights gained in past eras. Our understanding of ethics

Review: *Many Times and Many Places* by K. Alan Snyder and Jamin Metcalf

Josiah Peterson

History professor and Lewis scholar K. Alan Snyder (of PonderingPrinciples.com fame) teamed up with his former student and history-teacher-turned-pastor, Jamin Metcalf, to offer the first book dedicated to C.S. Lewis's thoughts on history. The book is a scholarly yet accessible apologetic for the study of history as an antidote to many modern ills.

The book's title, *Many Times and Many Places*, comes from Lewis's 1939 talk, "Learning in Wartime":

> Most of all, perhaps, we need intimate knowledge of the past... A man who has lived in many places is not likely to be deceived by the local errors of his native village; the scholar has lived in many times and is therefore in some degree immune from the great cataract of nonsense that pours from the press and the microphone of his own age.[1]

In this talk, Lewis treats history as a liberal art—a study that equips one for freedom. Snyder and Metcalf return to this point often while also exploring Lewis's credentials as a historian, his approach to the necessary evil of 'periodization', his critique of 'historicism', and how the proper study of history strengthens one's imagination. They also include a very long chapter examining every one of Lewis's fiction

---

1 C.S. Lewis, "Learning in Wartime" in *The Weight of Glory* (San Francisco: HarperCollins, 1980), 58-59.

works with regard to historical parallels (though not every book seems to warrant this treatment).

How is it that Lewis, the apologist, literature scholar, and fiction writer, comes to be treated as an authority on history? The authors make the case that Lewis's studies and his professional work more than qualify him to have an opinion on the discipline of history. His history tutor at Oxford, George Stevenson, said he had much promise as a scholar.[2] The history students he tutored spoke of his class as fertile training ground for their studies.[3] Much of Lewis's own scholarship hinged on reintroducing modern audiences to old ideas. Lewis wrote *A Preface to Paradise Lost*, *English Literature in the Sixteenth Century* (part of the *Oxford History of the English Language*), and *The Discarded Image* largely to reintroduce students to older philosophy and culture so they might understand their literary heritage.

Lewis's reintroduction work is necessary because of the vast cultural divide between modern readers and their pre-modern predecessors. Lewis argued that the major historical dividing line comes not between the Medieval and the Renaissance periods, as is sometimes supposed, but sometime shortly after the lives of Jane Austen and Walter Scott (late 18th, early 19th centuries). Quoting from Lewis's inaugural address upon taking the chair of Medieval and Renaissance Literature at Cambridge, *De Descriptione Temporum*":

> Roughly speaking we may say that whereas all history was for our ancestors divided into two periods, the pre-Christian and the Christian, and two only, for us it falls into three—the pre-Christian, the Christian, and what may reasonably be called the post-Christian.[4]

---

2 Snyder and Metcalf, *Many Times and Many Places*, 26.
3 An interview with historian A.G. Dickens, "Tutored by Lewis," is included as an appendix.
4 Lewis, *De Descriptione Temporum*, 5, quoted in Metcalf and Snyder, 40.

These post-Christians, Metcalf and Snider summarize, are inculcated into "a materialistic, naturalistic, and functionalistic understanding" of man and the universe with the result that modern students are alienated from the art and literature of the past.[5] Lewis thought recognizing the shift is an important part of checking its influence.

Lewis blames this shift on Darwinian assumptions of "progress" applied to human social development, reinforced by the observation of rapidly advancing technology over the 19th and 20th centuries. This leads modern man to assume that newer is always superior, an attitude Lewis calls "chronological snobbery." Modern education, which has largely removed older authors from the curriculum and only references them at all second hand, contributes to the assumption that we have nothing to learn from the past, other than perhaps to show how far advanced we are. Not too long ago it was commonly believed "that valuable truth could still be found in an ancient book."[6] Lewis himself had succumbed to "chronological snobbery," as he called it, from which he had to be rescued by the likes of G.K. Chesterton and Owen Barfield.[7]

The best way to remedy chronological snobbery, Lewis thought, was to read old books. But not just read to dissect them, but to see through the eyes of their authors. Or, to put it another way, one needs to imaginatively enjoy old books rather than merely ponder them. Snyder and Metcalf explore the theory and offer examples in their delightful chapter on "Historical Imagination." Reading old books requires humility and modesty, not trying to use the past like some sort of map or prophecy through which we can read the future of mankind

---

5 Metcalf and Snyder, *Many Times and Many Places*, 40.
6 Lewis, "Modern Man and his Categories of Thought," *Present Concerns*, quoted by Metcalf and Snyder on 99.
7 Snyder and Metcalf reference *The Everlasting Man* several times throughout the text and include an impressive section on Lewis and Barfield's "Great War" over the role of imagination in epistemology that is the best basic introduction to this debate that I've ever read.

(the error of the "historicist"), but humbly trying to understand it for what it is, a snapshot of a particular place and time. Such sympathetic reading expands the capacity of one's imagination, and while Lewis differed from Barfield about whether imagination was a source of truth, he agreed that it is essential for understanding.[8] Metcalf and Snyder leave nary an artifact unexamined in their efforts to compile Lewis's outlook on history. They comb through his letters, finding his commentary to his brother Warnie on reading Gibbons' *The History and Fall of the Roman Empire*, (no good, Lewis thought, as it perpetually judges the actions of historical figures by modern standards) and his delight in reading Herodotus and Tacitus—his "light" reading with his tutor, "the Great Knock."[9] [10] They even examine Lewis's marginalia from the books in his personal library, including various historical texts, archived at the Marian E. Wade Center at Wheaton College. They are up-to-date on very recent scholarship, such as David Baxter's *The Medieval Mind of C.S. Lewis* from 2022 and Jeffrey Barbeau's "C.S. Lewis and the Romantic Heresy" lecture from just last year. Yet they do not neglect classic Lewis scholarship such as Peter Schakel's *Reason and Imagination in C.S. Lewis: A Study in Till We Have Faces* from forty years ago.

While rigorous in scholarship, the style and manner are accessible. The book assumes more familiarity with Lewis on the part of its readers than it does the discipline of historical study. There are a few "as everyone knows" sorts of comments regarding Lewis's more popular works, but the authors are sure to define historical terms, concepts, and examples, and controversies with sufficient context so that readers can understand what's being talked about. Chapters can largely

---

[8] They don't shy away from the difficult topics, such as Lewis and Barfield's "Great War" over the epistemological role of the imagination, including references to Stephen Thorson's *The Poetic Imagination*.
[9] Snyder and Metcalf, *Many Times and Many Places*, 29, 17.
[10] C.S. Lewis, *Surprised by Joy* (New York: HarperCOllins, 2017), 162. Also the title of Chapter IX, beginning on p. 161.

stand alone, with points and sources being reintroduced each chapter. This produces some redundancies but not enough to be tedious.

Snider and Metcalf have opened wide a new vein for mining treasures out of Lewis studies, but perhaps even more significant have provided an exhortation to teach and engage history imaginatively. Readers would do well to follow up this new book with some Herodotus or the Venerable Bede.

From Medieval to Modern and Beyond

Seth Myers

When did modernity begin and exactly where did it come from? Answering these questions can be challenging. A brief list of key inventions which radically changed human experience helps to locate the onset of the era:

> **Gutenberg's printing press** (1440)
> **Steam engines** (1600s until James Watt's improvement of 1764 to help power ocean travel and the industrial revolution)
> **Electric machines** (Faraday, 1832; Siemens and Wheatstone, 1867, powering electricity consumption)
> **Telephone** (Alexander Graham Bell, 1876)
> **Automobile** (Henry Ford, Model T, 1908)
> **Transistor** (Bell Labs, 1947)
> **Digital computer** (Konrad Zuse, 1950)
> **Cell phone** (Motorola, 1973, weighing 4.4 lbs)

A more philosophical approach eyes the progression of historical eras—from the Ancients, all the way to Medievals, Renaissance, Reformation, Enlightenment, Romantics, Modernity, and Postmodernity.

Such lists help us to identify some key features of modernity: a scientific mindset, industrial and technological progress which helped to move us from the feudal past, societal changes such as increasingly representative government and a market economy which have allowed human flourishing (with admittedly colonial disparities) previously reserved for aristocratic classes, and a consumer society. Philosopher Charles Taylor thus succinctly characterizes modernity as an

Aquinas designated reason an activity of the intelligible soul.[7]

Two centuries later, Enlightenment era poet Alexander Pope similarly admitted the divine origins of human nature. In his *Essays on Man* (1732, 1734) (purposing to "vindicate the ways of God to man" just as Milton claimed to "justify the ways of God to man" in *Paradise Lost*), Pope claims man's glory derives from God, and his wretchedness from falling short of such, opening *Essay on Man: Epistle II* with,

> Know then thyself, presume not God to scan; The
>   proper study of mankind is man.
> Plac'd on this isthmus of a middle state, A being
>   darkly wise, and rudely great…
> He hangs between; in doubt to act or rest; In doubt
>   to deem himself a god or beast…
> Born but to die, and reas'ning err… Chaos of thought
>   and passion, all confus'd…
> Created half to rise, and half to fall; Great lord of all
>   things, yet a prey to all;
> Sole judge of truth, in endless error hurl'd: The
>   glory, jest, and riddle of the world![8]

J.R.R. Tolkien would echo the same refrain in the twentieth century, explaining in his poem 'Mythopoeia' (dedicated, in effect, to C.S. Lewis for his journey to faith) that,

> The heart of man is not compound of lies,
> but draws some wisdom from the only Wise,
> and still recalls him. Though now long estranged,
> man is not wholly lost nor wholly changed.
>
> Dis-graced he may be, yet is not dethroned,

---

7 Thomas Aquinas, *Summa Theologica in Great Books of the Western World* vol. 17 (Chicago: Encyclopaedia Britannica, 2003), J. Mortimer Adler Editor in Chief, Question LXXVIII, p. 414.
8 Alexander Pope, *An Essay on Man*: Epistle 1, l 16, https:/www.poetryfoundation.org/poems/44899/an-essay-on-man-epistle-I.

and keeps the rags of lordship once he owned,
his world-dominion by creative act:
not his to worship the great Artefact,

Man, sub-creator, the refracted light
through whom is splintered from a single White
to many hues, and endlessly combined
in living shapes that move from mind to mind.

Though all the crannies of the world we filled
with elves and goblins, though we dared to build
Gods and their houses out of dark and light,
and sow the seed of dragons, 'twas our right
(used or misused). The right has not decayed.
We make still by the law in which we're made.[9]

The "Reason" that such early modern writers found in man was paralleled by the order they found in the universe. Elizabethan poet Edmund Spenser imagined creation ordered by divine love, envisioning that

The earth the air the water and the fire...
conspire each against each other...
threatening their own confusion and decay.
Till Love relented their rebellious ire [10]

Sir John Davies saw not just divine order but a dance, when in *Orchestra* (1594) he penned that

The turning vault of heaven formed was,
Whose starry wheels he hath so made to pass
As that their movings do a music frame

---

9 J.R.R. Tolkien, *Mythopoeia*, 1931, https://www.tolkien.ro/text/JRR%20Tolkien%20-%20Mythopoeia.pdf.
10 Edmund Spenser, "Hymn of Heavenly Love" in *Four Hymns*, 1596 in Tillyard, *Elizabethan World Picture*, 12, https://allpoetry.com/An-Hymne-of-Heavenly-Love.

And they themselves still dance unto the same.[11]

Malcolm Guite explains that Davies displays

> a picture of the universe we inhabit animated by the double emblems of love and dancing... in which the traditional hierarchies and interconnections of the great chain of being, which can sometimes seem fixed, frozen and patriarchal in prose accounts, are all set in motion of delight, a dance that fallen man, if he could only purge himself sufficiently to hear the music, is invited to join.[12]

This view of the cosmos bequeaths its sense of order, dynamism, and even the rational nature of man to the Moderns. Such a modernity is, however, merely a model, which can become a "discarded image" (as Lewis puts it) just as did the Medieval model, best fit for explaining natural phenomena to its own generation, and thus subject to that generation's psychology or mentality. "Hardly any battery of new facts could have persuaded a Greek that the universe had an attribute so repugnant to him as infinity; hardly any such battery could persuade a modern that it is hierarchical," Lewis explains.[13]

Modernity's Starting and Finish Lines

Lewis placed the great divide in human history later than simply the climb out of the Medieval world (the "unchristening" of Europe), and even later than the Renaissance or the Elizabethans. When accepting the position of Chair of

---

11 *The Poems of Sir John Davies*, ed. R. Krueger (Oxford: Oxford University Press, 1975), verse 19. Online https://www.poetrynook.com/poem/orchesra-or-poem-dancing.
12 Malcolm Guite, *Faith, Hope and Poetry* (Surrey: Ashgate Publishing, 2014), 78.
13 C.S. Lewis, The Discarded Image: An Introduction to Medieval and Renaissance Literature (Cambridge: Cambridge University Press, 1995), 222.

Medieval and Renaissance Literature Studies at Cambridge University in 1954, Lewis cited another scholar who claimed that "As the Middle Ages and the Renaissance come to be better known, the traditional antithesis between them grows less marked."[14] Further, Medieval Christians and Ancient Pagans had more in common with each other than with Moderns Lewis claimed, as "the gap between those who worship different gods is not so wide as between those who worship and those who do not."[15] Lewis does offer the end of the Elizabethan era (end of Seventeenth century; a bridge from the Medieval to more modern eras) as yet another possible line of demarcation owing to the development of the natural sciences, though their influence on the various sciences of man (psychology, sociology, political and economic society) had to wait a few more centuries.

Lewis instead claimed the advent of modernity was much closer to the time of the Romantics of the early Eighteenth century, just after Jane Austen (1775-1817), and concurrent with the birth of machines. That is when the idea of incessant progress, which replaced that of valuing enduring and permanent things, fundamentally altered modern man's psyche. The continual expectation that what is new is better may be appropriate for technical progress, but leads to a fundamental loss of cultural treasures, as the Age of Machines and the Age of Darwin neatly coincided in erasing the mindset that saw wonder and purpose imbued in the cosmos.

That modernity began somewhere near the age of the Romantics is echoed by influential Christian philosopher Charles Taylor, who argued that the *expressive individualism* begun by Jean Jacques Rousseau (1712-1778) is a hallmark feature of the modern era. The culture of modernity was marked by an increase in sentiment fueled in parts by the advent of the modern novel glorifying the issues of mundane, everyday life (in contrast to, say, Bunyan's moralistic *Pilgrim's*

---

14 C.S. Lewis, "De Descriptione Temporum", 1.
15 Ibid.

Progress). Novels such as Rousseau's *La Nouvelle Heloise* (1761) and Goethe's *Sufferings of Young Werther* (1774) raised the importance of individual sentiment to new heights, in a manner similar to how the title of Augustine's faith-dominated *Confessions* was co-opted by Rousseau's 1770 autobiography featuring instead his personal feelings about daily experiences. The work of Enlightenment era physiocrats, such as moral philosopher and economist Adam Smith (*The Wealth of Nations*, 1776), further distanced the age from assumption of a divinely-guided cosmos, substituting instead a self-regulating, human system. But the key insight of Taylor for the opening divide of modernity is his claim of the age's *expressive individualism*. Medievals and even Enlightenment era Deists saw human beings set in a larger natural order, often conceived as a providential order with which they should be in harmony.[16]

By contrast the Romantics, theorists of the sentiments, from Rousseau onward and including Wordsworth, substituted the authority of feeling, however inspired by nature, for any external claims on us. Taylor explains,

> It is through our feelings that we get to the deepest moral and, indeed, cosmic truths... Novalis [says] "The heart is the key to the world and life"... if we think of nature as a force, an elan running through the world which emerges in our own inner impulses... then we can only know what [this force] is by articulating what these impulses impel to us... this is the view that I have called elsewhere "expressivism."[17]

Such "expressivism" is radically individualistic, inasmuch as every individual is unique. Individual giftedness for one's calling, one's vocation, is of course understood from St. Paul to the Puritans, Taylor observes, though, "what the

---

16 Taylor, Sources of the Self, 369.
17 Ibid., 371-374.

eighteenth century adds is originality... We are all called to live up to our originality... This has been a tremendously influential idea. Expressive individualism has become one of the cornerstones of modern culture.[18]

Man's view of his spiritual nature, and art itself, becomes fundamentally altered in modernity, as Taylor observes that "The expressive view of human life went along naturally with a new understanding of art... it has come to take a central place in our spiritual life, in some respects replacing religion. The awe we feel before artistic originality and creativity places art on the border of the numinous.[19] Taylor describes the shift in terms of one from *mimesis* to *poesis*:

> The traditional understanding of art was as mimesis. Art imitates reality... But on the new understanding, art is not imitation, but expression... The artist doesn't imitate nature so much as he imitates the author of nature... Herder puts it bluntly "The artist is become a creator God.[20]

Carl Trueman cites Taylor, explaining, "A mimetic view regards the world as having a given order and a given meaning and thus sees human beings as required to discover that meaning and conform themselves to it. Poiesis, by way of contrast, sees the world as so much raw material out of which meaning and purpose can be created by the individual.[21]

The divine dynamism of Davies's "dance of Love" animating the cosmos thus yields to an incessant march of technology, but it is a technology unaware of any sense of

---

18 Taylor, Sources of the Self, 376.
19 Ibid.
20 Ibid., 377-78.
21 Carl R. Trueman, *The Rise and Triumph of the Modern Self: Cultural Amnesia, Expressive Individualism, and the Road to Sexual Revolution* (Wheaton: Crossway Books, 2020), 39. Kindle. Trueman extends the point to today's sexual revolution of alternative sexuality, a case he claims of not accepting the world as given (mimesis) but attempting to make it according to individual desires (poesis).

wonder, meaning, or purpose in the cosmos. Further, technology often only delays or transforms, rather than actually solving, man's problems. For instance, the automobile replaced piles of horse dung on the streets with carbon emissions that now threaten the health of the planet. Similarly, social media's boon of instant global connectedness has also brought the bane of incivility, bullying, unprecedented access to morally unconstrained sexual practice, and fraudulent financial schemes. The limits of scientific and material progress echo those Pascal (1623-1662) declared of secular philosophy centuries earlier, declaring in his *Pensees,*

> It is in vain oh men, that you seek in yourselves the cures for your miseries.
> All your insights have led to the knowledge that it is not in yourselves
> that you discover the true and the good.
> The philosophers promised them to you, but they were not able to keep that promise,
> for they did not know what your true nature is, or what your true good is.
> How then could they have provided for you a cure for the ills they have not even
> Understood.[22]

Just as the march of technology has been problematic, so has the progression of civilizational eras only relocated, not solved, the problems of man. Enlightenment rationality and science paved the roads of understanding, civil discourse, and scientific and material progress, though mankind's wars intensified in the centuries that followed. England, the center of so much civic and industrial progress, democratic liberalism and the Industrial Revolution which continue to inspire democratic governments and lift tens of millions out

---

22 Blaise Pascal, *Pensees* (Oxford: Oxford University Press, 2008), trans. Honor A. Levi, XII, A.P.R. 54-55.

of poverty globally, praised itself in the Victorian era patriotic hymn composed for King Edward VII's 1901 coronation, "Land of Hope and Glory," with the chorus,

> Land of Hope and Glory, Mother of the Free
> How shall we extol thee, who are born of thee?
> Wider still and wider shall thy bounds be set;
> God, who made thee mighty, make thee mightier yet,
> God, who made thee mighty, make thee mightier yet.[23]

But such optimism came to a crashing halt early in the twentieth century with the Great War (WW1, 1914-1918) as William Butler Yeats opined that in *The Second Coming* (1921)

> Things fall apart; the centre cannot hold
> Mere anarchy is loosed upon the world
> The blood-dimmed tide is loosed, and everywhere
> The ceremony of innocence is drowned;
> The best lack all conviction, while the worst
> Are full of passionate intensity.[24]

The utter lack of confidence is echoed by T.S. Eliot's J. Alfred Prufrock who fearfully asks

> Do I dare
> disturb the universe?
> In a minute there is time
> For decisions and revisions which a minute will reverse.[25]

Eliot's "The Wasteland" poem of 1922, often hailed as the

---

23 "Land of Hope and Glory," music by Edward Elgar, lyrics A.C. Benson, 1902.
24 William Butler Yeats, "The Second Coming," 1919, https://www.poetryfoundation.org/poems/43290/the-second-coming.
25 T.S. Eliot, "The Love Song of J. Alfred Prufrock" in *T.S. Eliot: The Complete Poems and Plays 1909-1950* (New York: Harcourt, Brace & World Inc., 1971), 4-5.

inaugural work of twentieth century literary modernism, in which the Fisher-King figure (a wounded king whose lands suffer with him) dejectedly muses,[26] [27]

> Shall I at least set my lands in order?
> London Bridge is falling down falling down falling down
> These fragments I have shored against my ruins.[28]

Eliot does search throughout the poem for wisdom from Augustine and Buddha to manage man's burning desires which often engulf the world in literal flames, finally resorting to Hindu scriptures before coming to Christian faith a decade later, as expressed in such poems as The Four Quartets and Ash Wednesday.

Apogee of Modernity: Four Nineteenth Century Horsemen of the Anti-Transcendent, and the Path They Wander to Postmodernity

Just as the new atheism claims its own fourfold set of evangelizing equestrians—philosopher-scientists Richard Dawkins, Sam Harris and Daniel Dennett along with journalist Christopher Hitchens—so does modernity, with Charles Darwin, Sigmund Freud, Karl Marx, and Friedrich Nietzsche. But (long) before Darwin, Freud, Marx and Nietzsche, there was Plato, Markos reminds us, and he would have none of the radical empiricism of these nineteenth century "visionaries":

Before the nineteenth century, most Europeans

---

26 Russell Kirk, Eliot and His Age: T.S. Eliot's Moral Imagination in the Twentieth Century (Washington: Regnery Gateway, 2008), Digital edition.
27 Jeffrey M. Perl, *Literary Modernism: The Struggle for Modern History* (Springfield: The Teaching Company, 1997. Lecture series with course notes.
28 T.S. Eliot, "The Wasteland" in T.S. Eliot Complete Poems and Plays 1909-1950, 50.

possessed a worldview shaped by a theology grounded in the Bible and a philosophy that traced its roots back to Plato. Central to both of these traditions was a belief that the nature of reality was top to bottom. That is to say, the real, the essential, the original resided above in a spiritual heaven, while all that lay below in this physical, natural world was created by, descended from, or was an imitation of those original heavenly presences. The spiritual was the primary, the physical was the secondary.[29]

Such a top-down approach as Markos explains "logocentrism," and was the order of the day from Plato until the Christian poet Samuel Taylor Coleridge (poet and theologian/philosopher/literary critic, 1772-1834, key figure along with William Wordsworth of the Romantic movement). The apostle John adapted the Platonic tradition when declaring of Jesus, "In the beginning was the Word" (translated logos), the message of God communicated to humanity. Logocentrism has a long history with philosophers among others, as John's transcendent logos (Jesus) finds impersonal analogies with Plato's eternal, immutable "Forms," Hegel's "Idea," and even the transcendent "Ego" of psychologists. Logocentrism typically expresses itself through binaries, pairs in which the first term is the original, more pure or eternal form from which the second is derived, or even "falls away." Such pairs include soul / body, logos (word, logic, speech) / praxis (act, experience, writing), being / becoming, essence / existence, genius / art, intellectual / physical, rational / emotional, Apollonian / Dionysiac.[30] The second term of the binary relations suffer not just from lack of originality (as it were) but are marginalized as well; such are

---

29 Louis Markos, Lewis Agonistes: How C.S. Lewis Trains Us To Wrestle With The Modern And Postmodern World (Nashville: Broadman & Holman, 2003), 30.
30 Louis Markos, *From Plato to Postmodernism: Understanding the Essence of Literature and the Role of the Author,* Lecture Twenty-One: Origins of Modernism (Chantilly: The Teaching Company, 1999), Part 2, 44.

the claims of those who critique such historically practiced binary relations as male/female, white/non-white, and Western/non-Western; such "marginalization" occurs as the first term is considered central, and the second peripheral.

The disruption of two millennia of the logocentric tradition (though it had its rebels) began in the modern era with Charles Darwin (1809-1882) and Sigmund Freud (1856-1939). Darwin made the first and most obvious inversion of long-esteemed binaries, claiming that man was not descended from God (*imago Dei*, "in the image of God"), but instead evolved upward from apes. Freud continued this inversion, arguing that we simply project the idea of God from our needs, such as imagining a heavenly father simply to protect us from pain and suffering. Freud continued the reversal, as his practice of psychotherapy led to a privileging of the subconscious mind over the conscious mind (our beliefs, decisions), which was traditionally considered of primary importance. In reversing this binary claiming the unconscious mind was the true source of our (conscious) thoughts, Freud's influence led to neuroses becoming the norm for society, with normalcy the exception, so that we are as often as not viewed first as a bundle of some set of neuroses, Markos observes.

Philosophers Karl Marx (1818-1883) and Friedrich Nietzsche (1844-1900) completed the anti-logocentrism game begun by Darwin and Freud, explicitly declaring the transcendent, God himself in the case of Nietzsche, to be dead. Marx began his analysis with society, declaring that ideology and beliefs were most strongly influenced by the most materialistic aspect of society, specifically the economic means of production. Religious beliefs were a matter of class warfare rather than transcendent truth-claims, and any other activities such as art or one's own conscious understanding were as well bound to historical determination, affected only by one's place in society. Markos summarizes that for Marx, "economic means and the mode of production… formed a substructure on which all social, political, religious, and aesthetic thought rested."[31] French Philosopher Michel Foucault (1926-1984) would later advance Marx's thesis to indict vast networks of social power in determining one's beliefs. Friedrich Nietzsche was even more explicit, if not fevered, in declaring the death of truth itself (and God along with it). Truth is an illusion that man once created, but then forgot that he was its author; God is like such truth, in that the Europe of his day, Nietzsche claimed, had been effectively forgotten, we ourselves had killed off the idea. While Nietzsche is more famous for inverting the Apollonian/Dionysiac binary (truth and passion, as a simplification), in an essay "Truth and Falsity in an Ultramoral Sense" Nietzsche explicitly denies the existence of any logos, form, or truth. [32]

Theologians even partook in the anti-logocentrism game. "Higher Criticism," the radical branch of the Historical-Critical school of theology studies which otherwise sought to understand the Bible better in its actual historical context, typically denied divine origins of Scripture and deity itself. David Friedrich Strauss's *The Life of Jesus* (1846) denied the divine nature of Jesus posting instead the "historical Jesus," and Ludwig Feuerbach's *The Essence of Christianity* (1854) argued that God is merely a projection of man's best qualities, but not a separate being. Such works influenced Darwin, Freud, and Marx, with the theological controversy overshadowing in the 1860s the controversies from Charles Darwin's newly published *Origin of Species* (1859). Liberal Protestantism, begun with the works of Strauss, Feuerbach and before them Friedrich Schleiermacher (1768-1834), influenced later theologians such as Rudolf Bultmann (1884-1976) who sought to demythologize the historical biblical narratives, but also led Pope Pius X in 1907 to condemn such modernism as "the synthesis of all heresies."[33] Pope Paul VI

---

31 Markos, *Lewis Agonistes*, 34.
32 Markos, From Plato to Postmodernism, part 2, 47.
33 Pope Pius X, (8 Sept., 1907) "Pascendi Dominici Gregis," https://www.ewtn.com/catholicism/library/on-the-doctrine-of-the-modernists-3496.

would again condemn modernism in *Ecclesiam Suam* (1964). The modernist "higher criticism" approach affected scholarship of both the Old and New Testaments, as in the place of divinely-inspired Mosaic authorship of the books of the Pentateuch, four distinct, evolving phases of authorship were suggested (J,E, P, and D), while Paul's epistles and even John's gospel were claimed to have been developed over two centuries.[34] Similar efforts were applied to the works of Homer, such as the *Iliad* and *Odyssey*.

The modernist program carried over in the later twentieth century into Structuralism and finally into Postmodernism. Structuralism continued modernism's anti-logocentrism, asserting that consciousness is a by-product of social and even material conditions of life. Linguist Ferdinand de Saussure pioneered the structuralist perspective in his *Course in General Linguistics* (1913), as he argued that words refer not to predetermined transcendent concepts or meanings, but are arbitrarily determined by social processes. Anthropologist Claude Levi-Strauss adopted this approach in his anthropological studies, showing that social structures rather than free choices largely determine human behavior. Literary theorist Roland Barthes similarly argued that any meaning of a text is fabricated only by the "human process by which men give meaning to things," thus following Nietzsche.[35] French historian Michel Foucault practiced a structuralist analysis of history similar to Thomas Kuhn's paradigm shifts, with 'truth' simply being the adherence of some type of (typically coercive) discourse practice (political, sociological) with social facts, rather than alignment with a transcendent idea (as from religious belief or scripture).

Structuralists, at the tail end of modernity, provided passage to the postmodernity of the later twentieth century.

---

34 Markos, *Lewis Agonistes*, 37 -38. Markos notes that the discovery of Ryland Papyrus placed a section of John 18 clearly in the 90s A.D., refuting such efforts and presenting "clear proof that God has a sense of humor."
35 Markos, From Plato to Postmodernism, 50.

French-Algerian philosopher Jacques Derrida (1930-2004) broke down all sets of binary oppositions (soul/body, logos/experience, being/becoming, essence/existence) and thus all efforts to ground meaning in one extreme or the other, instead offering a free play of meaning amongst any and all participants. Even the structuralist's preferences for material conditions over ideological ones is a doomed effort, as it is impossible to ascribe any origin to meaning or to truth. Derrida argues that ever since Plato, over twenty-five hundred years ago, philosophers have naively sought to center meaning in a single, transcendent perspective. Derrida claims Nietzsche as an authority, given Nietzsche's claim that truth is constantly "in play." Nietzsche is thus foundational for both modernism and postmodernism. Freud did the same for any notion of a grounded, transcendental self. Further, existentialist Martin Heidegger argued against any pre-existent I AM of being (God or derivatively, man), following fellow existentialist Jean Paul Sartre who claimed that existence precedes essence.[36]

C.S. Lewis to the Rescue: Wrestling with Modernity

Markos's *Lewis Agonistes: How C.S. Lewis Can Train Us To Wrestle With The Modern and Postmodern World* opens by highlighting both the rational and the intuitive, myth- and story-loving aspects of the young Lewis. From a passionate, quixotic father and a cool, logical mother with a B.A. in math, to his iron-disciplined tutor, "The Great Knock," to his study of the classics, Lewis was equipped to wrestle with both the extreme rationalism of modernity as well as the spiritual appetites of the postmodern.

Lewis's conversion from modernist atheism to faith was led by his discoveries of what Markos describes as "things that

---

36 Markos, *From Plato to Postmodernism*, 50 for the overall paragraph of summary.

could not have evolved," phenomena not explicable by a purely rationalist, material account of reality. Markos elaborates four distinct steps, or components, of Lewis's approach.

The first were Lewis's experiences of "joy," nearly mystical moments of longing brought on by intimations of Autumn from Beatrix Potter stories or a flowering bush on a sunny day, as described in his autobiography *Surprised by Joy*. Desires which point beyond themselves and are not entirely quenched in this world led Lewis to formulate an "argument from desire," the idea that if we are not satisfied by this world we must have some transcendent, spiritual aspect.

Secondly, as he explained in the opening of *Mere Christianity*, the fact that when arguing about some matter, each opponent will typically appeal to some fundamental principle to which both claim to adhere (fairness or justice, for instance): this fundamental universal understanding of morality Lewis also claimed was given to humanity, not created by us, and he showed in his *Abolition of Man* how such ethical rules can be found in all cultures spread across both time and space.

Third, our ability to reason cannot be accounted for by simple natural processes: nature may exhibit regularities, but our minds are qualitatively distinct entities, and unlike lake algae or a flock of seagulls, able to formulate reasons of cause and effect that the objects of nature are unable to do themselves, as he argued in *Miracles*.

Fourthly and finally, human religion could not evolve on its own without some transcendent source. Comparing dread evoked by the numinous, say a ghost, is a different order than our fear that a tiger is in the next room (or put another way, men dread only skeletons of their own kind); when such moments of dread (or of the 'joy' he described earlier) are combined with the idea of universal morality, "religion" arises. Immoral religion (as often practiced in the ancient world) or nonreligious morality (the moral code of Buddhism is essentially atheistic) are worlds below that of a revealed religion such as Christianity which incorporates both aspects.

Such things "that could not have evolved" can be used to pose direct challenges to the modern. Of human morality, Markos compares the enduring commands of Jesus to Enlightenment era projects based on reason along, such as Kant's categorical imperative (treat everyone as you would like to be treated) which ultimately led in a single century's time to Nietzsche whose visions of an uberman-inspired Nazi Germany. Of scientific laws, things like the law gravity merely describe the process, not give the explanation, of phenomenon; as per *Miracles* a best explanation just may include a supernatural being who is able to suspend events to his will. Of joy and the argument from desire, Lewis provides a neat answer to Freud's charges of wish fulfillment or that natural instincts like lust explain the appearance of noble love: is it not possible that such lusts are merely a falling away from the higher form, sublime love? The dialogue between Eustace, Jill, and Puddleglum with the Emerald Witch in *The Silver Chair* shows the point, as the Witch offers that their idea of a sun outside the cave may just be their projections of the meager torches they know, to which Puddleglum retorts that even if their ideas of a sun and Narnia were unreal, they were preferred to the gloomy, meaningless world of the Witch's dark cavern.

The spiritual vacuum of the moderns thus naturally leads to the phenomenon of the postmoderns, which Markos equates with New Age spirituality. The "rejection of the excesses of modernism and materialism" has spurred an appetite which pursues spirituality in various non-orthodox forms such as Eastern religions, which typically draw from "the central element of paganism—pantheism."[37] Pantheism, the idea that the entire natural world is divinely composed, and its New Age format, can be simply seen as an effort to recapture the beauty, wonder, and enchantment in the world that the Medievals claimed centuries earlier! Lewis himself

---

37 Markos, *Lewis Agonistes*, 65, 63.

drew on the Medieval model, as presented above, in imbuing the worlds he created in his various fiction series, in the same way that Medieval poets like Dante, Chaucer, and Milton had done in their works. The Christian church needs to present the postmodern, New Age world with a world of wonder, meaning and significance, in a way the moderns could not, Markos argues. Just as the Magi seeking the manger were not Jews but likely Zoroastrians in pursuit of truth by the means they knew (star-gazing), so do we also need to combat the postmodern world's philosophical agnosticism, the idea that there are many truths, with the claim that "Christianity is not the only truth, but it is the only complete truth."[38]

Meeting the postmodern appetite for spirituality will require us to give Paul's message at Mars Hill to challenge the worshippers of lesser gods to complete their journey, and to point them towards the "mythical radiance resting on our theology… the heart of Christianity is a myth which is also a fact… [which] happens at a particular date, at a particular place, followed by definable historical consequences."[39]

Lewis demonstrated just how to rehabilitate this medieval perspective in his various works of fiction. In his *Space Trilogy,* this very anti-modernist is at the heart of its cosmos, as Ransom muses,

> He had read of 'Space': at the back of his thinking for years had lurked the dismal fancy of the black, cold vacuity, the utter deadness, which was supposed to separate the worlds. He had not known how much it affected him till now—now that the very name 'Space' seemed a blasphemous libel for this empyrean ocean of radiance in which they swam… Older thinkers had been wiser when they named it simply the heavens.[40]

---

38 Ibid., 72.
39 Markos, *Lewis Agonistes,* 72.
40 C.S., Lewis, *Out of the Silent Planet* (New York: Scribner, 2003), 34.

"If the space trilogy carries the medieval model up into the heavens, then the Chronicles of Narnia bring it back to the earth" Markos claims.[41] Aslan is God (Jesus, the Emperor lies in lands beyond the sea) ruling on Narnian earth, even reviving the land itself with his magic and his joy.

The problem of evil and suffering reveals another failing of the modernist program. Just as the logocentric worldview was fading in the eighteenth century, Rousseau replaced the traditional conception of man as sinful and in need of salvation with an optimism for the perfectibility of man. In place of the Christian view that our lust, pride, and disobedience lead us to rebel against God and his image in which we are made, for Rousseau it was society that corrupted man, and we need more natural sentiments to purify ourselves; such optimism fueled the reforms of the following centuries until they came crashing down to earth at the opening of the twentieth century. Lewis's *Problem of Pain* helps us out of this illusion, as in it he argues that real pain in this world results from God allowing us to bear the consequences of our choices (else they are not real choices at all). The pain we suffer is in fact a tool used by God to perfect our character, "we (like God) only discipline those whom we love" Markos adds, citing Lewis:

> For people for whom we care nothing... we demand happiness on any terms: with our friends, our lovers, our children, we are exacting and would rather see them suffer much than be happy in contemptible and estranging modes... He has paid us the intolerable compliment of loving us, in the deepest, most tragic, most inexorable sense.[42]

Lewis's own journey involved the pain of losing his wife Joy, as he came to admit that,

---

41 Markos, *Lewis Agonistes*, 85.
42 Markos, *Lewis Agonistes*, 99-100. From C.S. Lewis, *Problem of Pain*.

> Perhaps He had to destroy my image of Joy lest I make her into an idol that would block me from Him? God is, after all, the greatest of iconoclasts. He must shatter even our ideas of him, lest we worship the idea and not Him who is the origin of the idea.[43]

C.S. Lewis To the Rescue: Wrestling with Postmodernity

Markos does offer that John's gospel is a direct counter, a refutation, to the postmodern nihilism of Nietzsche and Derrida. "In the beginning was the Word [Logos], and the Word was with God, and the Word was God."[44] This clearly counters Derrida's famous claim that "there is no center," no origin, no fixed truth. Just as the Greek term of Logos represented the transcendent which they sought in reality, so Christ offers himself as that reality, "by whom and through whom [all of reality] was created." Fully appreciating the incarnation of Christ—God descent into the natural world—is key to answering the postmodern challenge; of it Lewis claimed, "The central miracle asserted by Christians is the Incarnation… It relates not a series of disconnected raids on Nature but the various steps of a strategically coherent invasion—an invasion which intends complete conquest and 'occupation'."[45]

The destruction of meaning due to "the 'logocidal' fury of the modern and postmodern world" implores the Christian to "cast our eyes backward to the medieval church and seek out a counter-vision of the arts," an "aesthetics of incarnation" where such meaning was unashamed to cavort with the created order's beauty.[46] The medieval tradition of artistic icons displays the significance of aesthetics. Markos explains

---

43 Markos, *Lewis Agonistes*, 108-109.
44 John 1:1 (NIV).
45 C.S. Lewis, *Miracles* (New York: HarperOne, 2015), 173.
46 Markos, *Lewis Agonistes*, 122.

that "The icon is a crux, an axis, a nexus at which the physical and spiritual, temporal and eternal meet… it is the very fact that God did take on flesh in the person of Christ that empowers the arts and enables them to strive toward the divine."[47]

It is not only graphic but verbal art that allows such ascension, as Markos further claims that "Poetry too, when it is most worthy of itself, is sacramental, striving ever to embody emotions and choices and struggles that can neither be seen nor heard nor tasted in words that are physical, tangible, consumable."[48] And it is not just art and poetry but the imagination as a whole in which such transcendent mystery can break through. Of Lewis's works of imaginative, "incarnational fiction," (*The Chronicles of Narnia*, the space trilogy, and *Till We Have Faces*) Markos declares that "Lewis constantly shifts between two realities that traffic back and forth as dramatically and dynamically as the angels descending and ascending on Jacob's Ladder.[49] Of the Chronicles, Markos claims, "Narnia and our own world are held up as icons of each other; in tracing Narnia's sacred history, we gain insight into our own narrative;" in the space trilogy, struggles in the physical and spiritual worlds are closely intertwined; in *Till We Have Faces*, "we enter fully into a pagan, pre-Christian tale in which every element of the story points in some way to Christ and to grace."[50]

The final way in which Lewis can speak to the "logocidal fury" of the modern and postmodern worlds is in its depiction of heaven and hell, the latter at least of which is anathema to this generation. That some go to hell while others arrive in heaven outrages the postmodern's sense of fairness, though it is more a matter of (divine) justice, Markos observes. Flattening historically preferred binaries, such as

---

47 Ibid., 126-127.
48 Ibid., 129.
49 Ibid., 134.
50 Markos, *Lewis Agonistes*, 134-135.

colonizers/colonized, is one of the virtues of the postmodern, but the idea of eternal inequality is thus even more repugnant. In *The Screwtape Letters* and *The Great Divorce*, Lewis shows that the choices between heaven and hell are being made continually. In this, Lewis follows Romantic poet William Blake's *Marriage of Heaven and Hell* (after which *The Great Divorce* is modeled) for whom heaven and hell were more a matter of our perception, and thus experience, of this world. In it, Blake anticipates Nietzsche in arguing that hell is simply being restrained from one's desires, and being restrained by those with stronger desires; Freud would follow in placing instinctual desires in the *id*, which wars with the moral conscience found in the *superego* until battles are resolved by the *ego*.

For Lewis, sin and the hell it creates here (a foretaste of the eternal) is a choice. Screwtape advises Wormwood,

> "You say these are very small sins... But do remember, the only thing that matters is the extent to which you separate the man from the Enemy [God]... Indeed, the safest road to Hell is the gradual one—the gentle slope, soft underfoot, without sudden turnings, without milestones, without signposts."[51]

Further, in tossing out the logocentric bathwater, the baby of our own humanity is lost. In *The Great Divorce* Lewis makes use of imagery in which the travelers on the bus ride from Hell to Heaven become more solid as they make heavenly choices, and more insubstantial and ghost-like otherwise; Hell itself turns out to fit between the blades of grass while Heaven is an expansive country. As Lewis articulates in *The Problem of Pain*, "To enter heaven is to become more human than you ever succeeded in being on earth; to enter hell, is to be banished from humanity."[52] Heaven in fact powers the

---

51 Markos, *Lewis Agonistes*, 153.
52 Ibid., 154.

artistic imagination, as it ennobles the human subject while exalting the divine. As Lewis explains in *The Great Divorce*, "When you painted on earth... it was because you caught glimpses of Heaven in the earthly landscape. The success of your painting was that it enabled others to see the glimpses too... He is endless. Come and Feed."[53]

Art, otherwise, becomes idolatry, exalting the merely human unmoored from its designer and author. Lewis's and Markos's final indictment of the merely human realm of the moderns and postmoderns is akin to the imagery of *The Great Divorce*, as our merely human desires (Freud, Nietzsche) are cast as not too strong but too weak for the things of heaven, as Lewis declares

> It would seem our Lord finds our desires not too strong, but too weak. We are half-hearted creatures, fooling about with drink and sex and ambition when infinite joy is offered us, like an ignorant child who wants to go on making mud pies in a slum because he cannot imagine what is meant by the offer of a holiday at the sea. We are far too easily pleased.[54]

The End of the Modern / Postmodern Story

A brief postscript on postmodernity is helpful, if only as an introduction to *An Unexpected Journal*'s forthcoming issue (Spring 2025) on postmodernity. Markos does observe that Derrida's nihilism is not, to Derrida anyway, a despairing one: instead, it is playful, looking to the future for determining meaning rather than looking back to an idyllic lost past, as with Rousseau, Wordsworth, Romantics and even Renaissance thinkers were wont to do.[55] Markos makes the

---

53 Ibid.
54 C.S. Lewis, "The Weight of Glory" in *The Weight of Glory and Other Essays* (New York: HarperOne, 2015), 26.
55 Markos, *Plato to Postmodernism*, "Lecture Twenty-Three "Derrida on Deconstruction."

parallel between Derrida and Sartre, for whom the absence of ultimate meaning made our choices even more important and vital (though ultimate despair is unavoidable).

Other Christian authors make similar points. In *C.S. Lewis and Christian Postmodernism: Word, Image, and Beyond* (2016) Kyoko Yuasa claims that Lewis, while anti-modernist, welcomes the more inclusive postmodern perspective, welcoming not just marginalized voices and cultures but that of the Christian voice, itself a myth like many others, but one with unrivaled power and historical claims. In her survey of the field, Yuasa cites several other Christian authors engaged with the postmodern approach. Crystal Downing (*How Postmodernism Serves My Faith*, 2006) claims that Derrida's "there is nothing outside of the text" claim merely resists modernist programs rather than meaning itself, and James K.A. Smith reinterprets Derrida within the context of Christian faith (*Who's Afraid of Postmodernism?* 2006).

In summary, to the modern Lewis reminds us of so much that cannot be explained by a purely material world, such as transcendent joy and desires not fully answered here, our sense of right and wrong, man's glorious faculties such as our ability to reason, and the revealed, Christian religion which unites both ethics and the numinous. To the postmodern whose cosmos has no transcendent center, Lewis offers God come to Earth, the eternal logos of Christ as that missing key, whose Incarnation thus models how we can show glimpses of the transcendent through art and imagination, recapturing the world of enchantment and beauty that the Medieval forbears to the Moderns once knew. Elizabethan poets and recent Christian scholars alike have been shown to provide a chorus of voices casting the Christian faith as a story with not just an actual history (which will be crucial when encountering the plethora of postmodern stories), but as a story with unique power—the power to enlighten, the power to enchant, and the power to redeem.

To Live Dangerously or Die Trying

Sarah Hadley

Happiness is something that can be found in the darkest of places. A dinner party amongst friends is often one of those happy places and not considered a dark place despite differing opinions that often arise. Opinions fill the pages of books in both fictional and non-fictional form on how to have a happy life. Here, an unwanted party guest attempts to defile an imaginative dinner party of classical thinkers who are presumably friends as they discover the happiness within.

As we completed dinner, I invited the guests to transition to the living room where we could sit comfortably around the fireplace and continue to enjoy the evening. Dr. Aquinas offered to help in clearing the table, claiming that we should all help one another so we could all enjoy the discussion at hand and not leave me to do it later or by myself even though I was the host. One could always count on Dr. Aquinas to serve his neighbor and fulfill the great commandment to love all. Mr. Kant and Mr. Goethe eagerly agreed and the three had all jumped in to clear the table before I could even disagree. We finished the table quickly and joined the others in the living room where we happened upon the special guest's controversial subject. Now to say he's *special* isn't to say that he has more or less meaning, or more or less worth. Mr. Nietzsche just happens to be a bit melodramatic and this dinner party was not intended for such flair. I simply wanted a quiet, peaceful dinner shared with friends, where we would break bread and share in thoughts and discussions, not a tense night, marked by the betrayal of peace. However, he showed up and I couldn't turn him out. Instead, I set another place and tried to be hospitable while walking on eggshells. What he meant for unsavory, we would try to make sweet.

So, here we were trying to have a peaceful, convivial evening when Mr. Nietzsche announced, "For believe me: the secret for harvesting from existence the greatest fruitfulness and the greatest enjoyment is—to live dangerously!"[1] Now, with any other crowd, this might have gone unscathed, unnoticed, and just disappeared into the night with the many comments floating around the room and the chosen drinks from dinner and after, but from this man, in this time, with this particular group of chosen dinner guests, there was no stopping the thoughts and opinions. The bread had been taken, the wine had been shared but the thirty pieces of silver were already in hand, pocketed, simply waiting for the kiss.

Mr. Aquinas had already made his way across the room to sit beside the kind-eyed, interesting Mr. Fyodor Dostoevsky, and they both sat silently staring into the fire. Mr. Lucretius was standing near the fire warming his hands but nearly dropped his cigar from the exuberant exclamation by Mr. Nietzsche, if it was from the shock of the volume or from the statement itself, I cannot be sure. I continued searching the room for responses as Mr. Kant, Mr. Goethe, and I awkwardly walked to the open seats in the silent room. A dropped pin could have been heard were it not for the creaking of the floors or the cracking of the fire, or Mr. Lucretius's long, wet drags on his cigar. I, like any good host, started to break the awkward silence that had infiltrated the room but was taken aback by Mr. Dostoevsky's face. It seemed absent and stern yet expressed a sense of inquisitive love that stopped me in my tracks. So, the discomforting silence continued to permeate the room. No one made eye contact as Mr. Nietzche's delighted gaze burned on each individual. His eyes reflected the flames

---

1 Friedrich Nietzsche, *The Gay Science, With a Prelude in Rhymes and an Appendix of Songs,* trans. Walter Kauffmann (New York: Knopf Doubleday Publishing Group, 1974), 228.

in the room and you could see beads of sweat arousing on his brow, while those he intended to rattle sat unfazed, contemplating, unsure of this conversation. Just as politics and religion are ill suited for certain groups, perhaps happiness, love, and demeanor were also taboo conversations for a dinner party.

As the antique grandfather clock chimed to inform us of the time, Mr. Lucretius paced to the rhythm like an anxious dog circling to get comfortable, he then found himself a chair as the last dong echoed through the room. Almost as abruptly and sharply as Mr. Nietzsche's first declaration, Mr. Lucretius settles in the chair then declares, "No report of gods, no lightning-flash, no thunder-peal made this man cower, but drove him all the more with passionate manliness of mind and will."[2] There was no turning back now, several were engaged, the conversation heightened. The peacefulness that had accompanied our dinner was now gone and it seemed the boxing gloves were coming out and we were all thrown into the ring together as Mr. Nietzsche sat with a certain smirk knowing his success in insinuating the friendly feast, the kiss had sealed the fate, but whose fate was still in question.

Mr. Lucretius voiced his thoughts on fear, declaring that it "induces hate of life and light, and men."[3] But before he could finish, Mr. Goethe interrupted, "Good, sensible people often withdraw from one another because of secret differences, each becoming absorbed by what he feels is right and by the error of the other. Conditions then grow more and more complicated and exasperating, until it becomes impossible to undo the knot at the crucial moment on which everything depends."[4] Leery of the conversation I spoke up, "Yes! Yes! If we are to go through with this conversation, what of the repercussions? Rifts created that are irreparable.

---

2 Lucretius, *The Way Things Are: The De Rerum Natura of Titus Lucretius Carus*, trans. Rolfe Humphries (Bloomington: Indiana University Press, 1968), 21.
3 Ibid., 88.
4 Johann Wolfgang von Goethe, *The Sorrows of Young Werther and Selected Writings*, trans. Catherine Hutter (New York: Signet Classics, 1962), 122.

Friends, should we? Dare we go on with this discussion?" Mr. Kant spoke directly to Mr. Goethe, "We shall be fine, good friends, as long as we use our logic. When we develop this reasoning and thought, it is an enlightenment that is expressed through independence of our thoughts and to our community which is one another."[5] So, there we had it. I got up to refill drinks and the conversation continued with the chosen few, except Mr. Dostoevsky who sat still and silent, staring into the fire.

"Each of us are masters of our own actions through reason and will," stated Dr. Aquinas, "Living dangerously with or without fear or love is still dangerous living. What is the difference between these? Is it not lustful and evil living that affects our living most?"[6] Mr. Lucretius had put down his cigar and was adamantly talking with his hands, "For all their excessive appetite for life, their cowardly fear of death—their unconcern became a Nemesis... The most pitiful thing of all was desperation, loss of nerve!"[7] I moved my gaze to look at Mr. Nietzsche's expression. It wasn't clear if he was enjoying the discussion or had drifted away into his own thoughts as his eyes had glazed and he was watching the fire. Abruptly Mr. Goethe spoke, "We yearn to surrender all of our Self and let ourselves be filled to the brim with a single, tremendous, magnificent emotion," he paused and rose to walk across the room to fetch himself a cigar, "we hurry to the spot, when there," (gesturing back to his seat) "becomes here, everything is as it was before and we are left standing in our poverty and constraint, our souls longing for the balm that had eluded us."[8] A new silence enveloped the room as the souls sat absorbed in their own emotional ties to longing. I was shaken from my comforting thoughts as I realized that Mr.

---

5 Immanuel Kant, "What is Enlightenment?", in *The Portable Enlightenment Reader*, ed. Isaac Kramnick (New York: Penguin Books, 1995), 6.
6 Thomas Aquinas, *Summa Theologica*, trans. Fathers of the English Dominican Province (New York: Benzinger Brothers, 1911-1925), I-II, q. 1, a. 1; I-II, q. 95, a. 1.
7 Lucretius, *The Way Things Are*, 234.
8 Goethe, The Sorrows of Young Werther, 42.

Dostoevsky was still quiet. It was unlike him to shy away from a hearty debate and discussion. I wondered where his thoughts were and made a mental note to ask him later if he never opened up to the conversation.

Dr. Aquinas, who had such a calm manner of speaking, broke the silence once again, "So, would we all agree that human actions therefore must be for an end?"[9] Sounds of agreement filled the room as he continued, "So, then we might all agree that happiness and satisfaction would be important in our living?"[10] Again, more nodding and grunts of approval, which I welcomed as the congenial host, as the Doctor continued by asking how virtue fit into the discussion. It was here I knew we had some vastly varying sentiments toward virtue and the conversation needed to shift to more agreeable discussions, "Virtue, oh must we really go there?" Mr. Goethe cheerfully sanctioned, "If only man would tell himself daily: you owe your friends nothing but to leave them their joys and increase their happiness by sharing it with them."[11] Good ol' Mr. Goethe. Kind, wise, Mr. Goethe.

"Yes, yes!" agreed Mr. Kant, "we need peace and unity among us, not things of strife; but I do think it's good to have an understanding amongst us, wouldn't you agree Mr. Nietzsche?"[12] As we all turned to where Mr. Nietzsche had been sitting, we noticed the emptiness on his face. The smirk that had been present, the sneering eyes, and unpleasant expression had faded, he sat motionless and slightly slouched. It is here that Mr. Dostoevsky silently crossed the room, suspecting something that none of us had noticed. He put his finger against the neck of Mr. Nietzsche then pronounced him dead. Shaking his head Mr. Dostoevsky solemnly reflected, "I heard a man once say, 'I live out my days in a corner, taunting myself with the spiteful and entirely useless consolation that

---

9 Aquinas, *ST* I-II. Q1. A1.
10 Aquinas, *ST* I-II. Q5.
11 Goethe, The Sorrows of Young Werther, 47.
12 Immanuel Kant, "Perpetual Peace," in *The Portable Enlightenment Reader*, ed. Isaac Kramnick (New York: Penguin Books, 1995), 553-559.

an intelligent man cannot seriously become anything and that only a fool can become something… Man only likes to count his troubles; he doesn't calculate his happiness. If he figured as he should, he'd see that everyone gets his share.'"[13] Mr. Dostoevsky crossed the silent room. He picked up his belongings, faced his companions who sat in disbelief, bowed his head and exited the party into the star lit streets.

---

13 Fyodor Dostoevsky, *Notes from Underground*, trans. Michael R. Katz (New York: W. W. Norton, 2022), 7, 103.

The Groundwork of Secularism: The Gifts of Modernity

Joshua Jo Wah Yen

The 19th century was a breakthrough period for secularism. Many thinkers like D.F. Strauss, C. Darwin, L. Feuerbach, and more made their major contributions towards secularism. While the arguments they made were not new, their impact on a societal and intellectual aspect allowed them to present a positive case for secularism in a way which has not been done before.[1] By understanding the arguments of these 19th century thinkers, one would be better equipped at interacting with secular peers, and also in recognizing the hidden arguments and motivations behind common atheist arguments. Therefore, this article is written with the goal of analyzing the works of Darwin, Feuerbach, Marx, and Strauss in order to provide the reader with this crucial insight into apologetics and contemporary debates about religion.

Darwin, Evolution, and the Relationship between Faith and Science

By positing that complex life forms, including humans, could emerge via natural processes, Darwin's theory of evolution challenged the foundations of the Christian faith. Firstly, if evolution is true, a literal, seven day creationist account of Genesis would be false, challenging the status and interpretation of Scriptures. Secondly, if God did not create man and humans are the result of materialistic processes,

---

[1] Most of the 19th century could be understood as responding to the philosophical contributions of Kant and Hegel.

then the belief that humans have intrinsic value given to them by a divine creator, would be undercut. The most notable challenge, however, was the conflict between faith and science.

Through Darwin's provision of an alternative hypothesis of how life came to be, Christians were challenged with how they should approach the conflicting creation narratives. For these reasons, both New Atheist thinkers like Richard Dawkins and fundamentalist Christians like Ken Ham have recognized evolutionary theory as a powerful argument against the Christian faith. Due to modern popularization of evolution as an argument against religion, it is tempting to assume that the image of the conflict between evolution and Christianity can be applied to the 19th century.[2] [3] [4] However, it is fascinating to note that the landscape of the 19th century was more nuanced and the growing movement of liberal Christianity made many Christians open to evolution, and in extension the sciences, as a way to further religious understanding.[5] In this section, I will examine two positions commonly held by 19th century Christians on the relationship between faith and science. By doing so, one would be able to recognise the historical precedence behind the conflict that many Christians experience today.

Compatibilist Presentations

Compatibilism states that while there may be superficial disagreements between faith and science, both fields, although different in methodology, work towards the same

---

[2] See Richard Dawkins, *The Blind Watchmaker* (New York: W.W. Norton & Company, 2015).
[3] See the debate between Ken Ham and Bill Nye. Ken Ham and Bill Nyc, "Bill Nye Debates Ken Ham," Creation Museum, February 4, 2004, YouTube video, https://www.youtube.com/live/z6kgvhG3Akl?si=Q2bOM6p6TvwCo-oG.
[4] Peter J. Bowler, "Christian Responses to Darwinism in the Late Nineteenth Century," in *The Blackwell Companion to Science and Christianity,* ed. JB Stump and Alan G Padgett (Sussex: Blackwell Publishing Ltd, 2012), 37.
[5] One must not conflate 19th century liberal protestant theology with modern conceptions of liberal Christianity.

truth. Therefore, established truths in theology or science could be used as tools to study the other. The tendency towards compatibilist interpretations of the 19th century could be explained by the influence of natural theology on Christian thought. Proponents of natural theology believed that order in the natural world pointed towards a "divine orderer of revealed religion."[6] As such, scientific and religious truths cannot be separated. Therefore, when the theory of evolution was presented by Darwin, many Christians, believing that science was a tool to enhance religious knowledge, attempted to incorporate evolution into their understanding of Christianity.[7]

However, adhering to compatibilism need not imply an acceptance of Darwinian evolution. Compatibilists like Otto Zöckler and Charles Hodge rejected Darwinian evolution yet adhered to the tenets of compatibilism.[8] To them, superficial disagreements between the fields of science and religion only arose due to the fallibility of the human mind which results in the distortion of both theology and science.[9] Rather, if one was given perfect rationality, one would be able to look beyond these disagreements and achieve a higher truth without contradiction. In fact, such an argument is not far from the argument of modern fundamentalist Ken Ham, who in his debate against Bill Nye, suggested that truth encapsulates all forms of knowledge, thus supporting the indistinguishability of science and religion.[10]

---

6 Matthew D. Eddy, "Nineteenth-century Natural Theology" in *The Oxford Handbook of Natural Theology*, ed. Russell Re Manning (Oxford: Oxford University Press, 2013), 104-105.
7 James C. Livingston, "Natural Science and Theology" in *The Blackwell Companion to Nineteenth Century Theology*, ed. David Fergusson (Sussex: Blackwell Publishing Ltd, 2010), 143.
8 Of course, it is important to note that Darwinian evolution was not proved irrefutably, rather there was still on-going scientific discourse on the topic.
9 Livingston, "Natural Science and Theology" in *The Blackwell Companion*, 152-154.
10 Ken Ham is a fascinating example of compatibilism. In theory, he is a compatibilist, believing that science and religion work hand in hand. However, in

Other compatibilist theologians of the 19th century like James McCosh made the argument that both religious truth and evolution can be compatible with each other. To McCosh, evolution did not disprove divine agency; rather, even if evolution was random, its prevalence in nature showed that it was not an accident.[11] Of course, such an argument would still mean a non-literal interpretation of the Genesis creation account, as a fundamentalist interpretation of Genesis would still entail a Young Earth model which would be incompatible with the timespan required for evolution. However, to give credit completely to Darwin for the movement away from literal interpretations of Genesis would be mistaken. It is important to recognize that many early church Fathers, like Augustine, promoted old earth interpretations of Genesis and many Christians at the time were also moving away from literal interpretations of the Genesis creation account due to a growing recognition of the existence of death prior to the fall and growing developments in geology.[12] From this brief outline of compatibilist positions held by Christians of the 19th century, one can appreciate how modern treatments of the relationship between faith and science have their roots in the 19th century.

Incompatibilist Presentations

The incompatibilists on the other hand were afraid that in the attempt to accommodate and synthesize both science and religion, one ends up distorting both the scientific and theological analysis.[13] Believing that science and religion had different goals and scope, incompatibilists often concluded

---

practice, one could argue that he is an incompatibilist as he presupposes religious and scriptural truth as the first point of reference such that any scientific theory can be judged based on the scriptures.

11 John H. Brooke, "Evolution and Religion" in *The Oxford Handbook of British Philosophy in the Nineteenth Century,* ed. W. J. Mander (Oxford: Oxford University Press, 2014), 214-215.

12 Ibid., 219.

13 Livingston, "Natural Science and Theology" in *The Blackwell Companion*, 148.

that there was not a unified 'higher truth' that science and religion work towards. As a result, many incompatibilists believed that it was best to separate the two fields for a more pure, unadulterated, and productive inquiry.

One advocate of incompatibilism was Baden Powell who argued that science should be allowed to have authority over the interpretation of the physical world whereas religion should be in charge of moral laws.[14] The distinction that Powell makes between the physical world and the moral law is representative of growing concerns in post-Darwinian society of the moral implications of evolution. If humans evolved, our notions of morality would likewise have evolved based on their reproductive advantages.[15] An evolutionary model of morality would have drastic impacts on the conception of the intrinsic value of human life, presenting a problem for anyone in support of a moral society, religious and atheist alike.

Another reason for incompatibilism stems from the challenge evolution presented towards the veracity of the Bible. Many denominations, especially Protestants, advocated a literal interpretation of the Genesis accounts, making evolution problematic as it provided an alternative hypothesis for creation.[16] To these Christians, any scientific hypotheses which contradicted their interpretation of scripture should lead to a rejection of the scientific hypothesis. Under the incompatibilist lens, Christians which attempt to update their theological viewpoints based on scientific developments make a methodological error and diminish the significance of Scripture by prioritizing non-Christian evidence. Since the 19th century, most Christians have moved away from the incompatibilist position with those who held to theological beliefs in conflict with the contemporary scientific consensus attempting to argue against Darwinism on scientific grounds.

---

14 Brooke, "Evolution and Religion" in *The Oxford Handbook*, 214.
15 Michael Ruse, "Evolution and Ethics in Victorian Britain" in *The Oxford Handbook of British Philosophy in the Nineteenth Century,* ed. W. J. Mander (Oxford: Oxford University Press, 2014), 244.
16 Ruse, "Evolution and Ethics in Victorian Britain" in *The Oxford Handbook,* 233.

Despite the movement away from incompatibilism, the relationship between science and faith remains an important question for all Christians to consider.

The Inheritance of Darwinism

Darwinian evolution created a formidable challenge to how Christians approached the relationship between science and faith. While many Christians adopted a compatibilist position, viewing science as a helpful tool in uncovering truth, many Christians maintained an incompatibilist position, fearing that advancements in science might undermine their faith and so rejected such fields altogether.

However, the conflict between faith and science was not the only aspect of Christianity that Darwinian evolution challenged. A further challenge of evolution was nihilism. If God does not exist, then neither do any higher sources of value; man is left alone in a material universe with no governing authority. However, with the growing threat of nihilism came a unique and eloquent voice, that of Ludwig Feuerbach, who argued that even though God did not create man, man did create God, and in the act of creation proved his own infinite potential.

Feuerbach, Religious Anthropology, and The Divinity of Man[17]

Compared to Marx or Darwin, Ludwig Feuerbach is a name that may be unfamiliar to many in the 21st century. However, *The Essence of Christianity* proved to be one of the most influential works of the 19th century, with Karl Marx describing him as "the only person who has a serious and a critical attitude to the Hegelian dialectic and who has made real discoveries in this field."[18] Feuerbach's argument was

---

17 It is important to note that Feuerbach wrote prior to the publication of Darwin's *On the Origin of Species*.
18 Karl Marx, "Critique of Hegel's Dialectic and General Philosophy" in *Marx on Religion*. Edited by John C. Raines. (Philadelphia: Temple University Press, 2002),

original as it challenged Christianity by demonstrating that religious belief can be reduced to a projection of human self-consciousness, successfully laying out the groundwork for materialism.

Religion as Anthropology

The uniqueness of Feuerbach's argument stems from his attempt to refocus the study of religion away from theology, an study of the nature of God, towards anthropology, a study of the nature of man.[19] Based on his anthropology, Feuerbach makes a positive case for atheism by arguing that religion is by nature atheistic and humanistic.[20] Religion is atheistic because it demonstrates that man is the creator of all things supernatural and humanistic because it exposes the infinite consciousness of man.

Feuerbach criticizes religion as an alienating force because it externalizes the properties of man to an external being—God—separating humans from their own potential and ability. Therefore, although the contents of religion may not be bad, its embodiment in theism oppresses the human spirit.[21] By arguing that God is the projection of human consciousness, Feuerbach states that man's infinite consciousness exalts man to God.[22] Feuerbach's argument may appear a stretch, but it is not without reason. If an effect can be no greater than its cause, man's act of creating God, psychologically, leads to the psychological deification of man.[23] The negation of the existence of God, as an external being, is expressed as the positive expression of the human condition, affirming humans as God, a godhood which was

---

77.
19 Feuerbach, The Essence of Christianity, 152.
20 Van A. Harvey, *Feuerbach and the Interpretation of Religion.* (Cambridge: Cambridge University Press, 1995), 2, 25.
21 Alasdair C. MacIntyre, *Marxism and Christianity.* 2nd ed. (London: Duckworth, 1995.), 26-27.
22 Feuerbach, The Essence of Christianity, xii.
23 Ibid., ix.

not something external, but rather internal.[24]

To illustrate Feuerbach's argument, I turn to the character Kirillov in Dostoevsky's *Demons*. Kirillov, as Paul Ramsey notes, recognised that

> "when God is dead, at the same instant [man] becomes God himself; and when one is like God, fully free, at the same instant he dies, being no longer bound to accept the conditions of his own existence."[25]

Without God, man becomes the only arbitrator of good and evil, becoming a God to himself. However, such divinity also comes with great responsibility, a burden which one cannot bear, leading to Kirillov's suicide. Through Kirillov, one is able to recognize the underlying movements of Feuerbach's philosophy and further appreciate the consequences of presenting God as a mere projection of the human mind.

Feuerbach is a religious anthropologist who argued for a reciprocal relationship between the properties of God and those of man. Since God is the projection of the human consciousness, every attribute bestowed upon God is a reflection of man's own attributes.[26] As such, the universal God is a representation of the group of its worshippers, and the personal God the representation of the individual.[27] By studying how one presents God, one would be able to

---

24 Marx's analysis of Feuerbach is worth quoting in full, "[Feuerbach has] opposed the negation of the negation, which claims to be the absolute positive, the positive which is based upon itself and positively grounded in itself." (Critique of Hegel's Dialectic, 77).
25 Paul Ramsey, "No Morality without Immortality: Dostoevski and the Meaning of Atheism," *The Journal of Religion* 36, no. 2 (1956): 93, http://www.jstor.org/stable/1199955.
26 One can see the similarities that Feuerbach's ideas had with the thought of Lacan.
27 Feuerbach, *The Essence of Christianity*, 90. "Your personal God is nothing else than your own personal nature."

understand the people who believed in that God. In Feuerbach's schema, it was not the death and resurrection of Christ which was divine, but rather the love that Christ's sacrifice represented.[28] The worship of Christ's resurrection discloses the omnipotence of human love and the power that humans have over the forces of evil in the world. Thus, by basing religion on anthropology, Feuerbach transforms God into an anthropological tool for illuminating human nature.

Feuerbach's Mantle of Divinity

It could be surprising that despite Feuerbach's materialism, his argument is profoundly spiritual. Feuerbach did not argue for the eradication of Christianity. Rather, he intended to uncover the essence of Christianity to facilitate a more critical understanding of religion. Feuerbach makes it clear that he does not end his argument with the rejection of God, as the New Atheists and secularists often do. Rather, he argues that man is God just as God is man.[29] Since Christianity is merely a projection of what is divine about mankind, to eradicate religion would be counterproductive. Rather, the proper treatment of religion in Feuerbach's system is to affirm their values as they express what is best about mankind.

Another valuable contribution of Feuerbach was his humanism. As noted in my examination of Darwin, one of the biggest challenges of the 19th century was the status of man in a godless universe. Feuerbach responds to nihilism in an ingenious way by arguing that the universe is not "godless." In a non-traditional way, gods do exist, because we are gods. While Feuerbach fails to touch on the potential dangers of man's newfound divinity as presented by Dostoevsky's Kirillov, Feuerbach nevertheless provides a structure in which human dignity is maintained through man's infinite consciousness. Metaphysicians may find this statement absurd, it is metaphysically impossible for man to become god

---

28 Harvey, *Feuerbach*, 47.
29 Ibid., ix.

or develop a god-essence. However, we need to recognise that Feuerbach, alongside other 19th century thinkers, were writing in a post-metaphysical world established by Kant where metaphysical objects are inaccessible by human reason alone.[30] Therefore, it is the infinite consciousness of humans which lies in the core of man's claim for meaning.

From Feuerbach, one can see how his argument was greatly influential to the 19th century and beyond. He did not intend to blindly do away with religion. Rather, he recognized the role of religion as projections of man's most fundamental desires and attributes. By doing so, Feuerbach not only introduced a novel interpretation of religion, but also provided a special role for humans in the universe, a groundwork for later developed by existentialist thinkers like Sartre. However, the role of man was not the only question secularism posed. Another prominent challenge was the interpretation of Scripture. There are few who could be considered as influential as D.F. Strauss whose mytho-poetic exegesis transformed Biblical criticism.

David Friedrich Strauss, Scripture, and His Mytho-poetic Exegesis[31]

David Friedrich Strauss's publication of *The Life of Jesus Critically Examined* made him one of the most prominent theologians of the 19th century. Like Feuerbach, D.F. Strauss did not aim to do away with religion, but to critically analyze its foundations. D.F. Strauss was not the first to criticize literal interpretations of the Scriptures; however, he was the culmination of a long line of criticisms and challenges, bringing to the forefront a refined model of liberal Biblical exegesis. Strauss argued that Biblical exegesis underwent four modes, a supernaturalist exegesis, a naturalist exegesis, a rationalist exegesis, and finally, a mythological exegesis. By

---

30 Pamela Sue Anderson and Jordan Bell, *Kant and Theology* (London: T & T Clark, 2010), 56.

31 Much of the information presented in this section is based on the lecture provided by Joel Rassmuesen at the University of Oxford.

analyzing the first three, it would help contextualize the landscape in which Strauss was writing and demonstrate the influences of modern Biblical criticism.

Movements in Critical Biblical Exegesis[32]

As the name suggests, the supernaturalist exegesis presupposes that the Bible was written in a supernatural world and was open towards supernatural accounts like miracles. Based on these presuppositions, adherents of the supernaturalist exegesis tend to adhere to more literal interpretations of Scripture. Although seemingly straightforward, the supernaturalist exegesis covers a spectrum of positions. On one side, the position held by Young Earth Creationists who hold to a literal interpretation of Biblical texts, and on the other side, those who, like Origen and Augustine, accept miraculous events, yet believed in symbolic and poetic interpretations of Scripture.[33] In the pursuit of a rigorous historical study of the Bible without the presupposition of faith, Strauss argued that it was necessary to move away from the model of divine intervention held by the supernaturalists towards historical exegesis.[34]

The naturalist exegesis is the opposite to the supernaturalist exegesis. Acting on the presupposition of a naturalistic world, the naturalist denies any account of the miraculous or the supernatural. Good examples of the naturalist position were the deistic naturalists of the 17th and 18th century like Toland and Bolingbroke who viewed the Bible as ridiculous and unbelievable. Furthermore, in a proto-Marxian way, Reimarus further argued that the Bible was an

---

32 I am defining liberal exegesis as the movement away from literal interpretations.
33 The reason why I raise Origen and Augustine is due to the common misconception that less literal interpretations was only a reactionary response to modernity and discoveries in science. Rather, these movements predated Darwin and other scientific judgment, providing further credence on potential non-literal exegesis.
34 David Friedrich Strauss, *The Life of Jesus Critically Examined*, trans. George Eliot (London: SCM Press, 1973.), 39.

artful deception to further political goals. As one can see, the naturalist exegesis does not only challenge the Bible on account of its supernatural accounts, but also attempts to present the Bible as a product of maliciousness or stupidity. Despite being a product of the 17th-18th century, it is remarkable to see how naturalistic exegesis had a short revival during the rise of New Atheism. However, just as New Atheism has since died down in popularity, the naturalist exegesis of the 17th-18th century was quickly replaced with what Strauss labeled the rationalist exegesis.

The rationalist exegesis noted the difficulties of a literal interpretation yet refused to be as harsh as the naturalists in their criticism of Scripture. According to the rationalists, by recognizing that Scripture was written in a former age, one should aim to translate the moral of the story to our modern times. While Kant was not a rationalist in a philosophical sense, his theological views embody the rationalist exegesis.[35] Kant placed the emphasis on Christ's moral actions instead of his divinity, writing that whether Christ is divine or not "can in no way benefit us practically, inasmuch as the archetype which we find embodied in this manifestation must, after all, be sought in ourselves."[36] and that "such a godly-minded teacher [Jesus], even though he was completely human, might nevertheless truthfully speak of himself though the ideals of goodness were displayed incarnate in him."[37] From these statements, one concludes that Kant is less worried about the metaphysical claims of Christianity, but its contribution towards fulfilling a higher moral archetype, which is for Kant the Categorical Imperative.[38] While Kant is a very good example of the rational exegesis, the scope of the rationalist

---

35 This is not to mention the general influence that Kantian philosophy had on 19th century protestant liberal theology, especially embodied in the Ritschlian school.
36 Immanuel Kant, *Religion Within the Limits of Reason Alone*, trans. Theodore M. Greene and Hoyt H. Hudson (Harper Torchbook, 1960), 57.
37 Kant, Religion Within the Limits, 54, 59.
38 God is one of the three postulates of the categorical imperative.

exegesis often varied. While many, like Kant, applied the rationalist exegesis to both the New and Old Testament, other thinkers like Eichhorn argued that while one should be critical of the Old Testament, one cannot likewise apply such an analysis to the New Testament without fundamentally altering the essence of Christianity.

Strauss and the Mythopoetic Exegesis

While Strauss rejected both the supernaturalist and the naturalist positions, he found himself in line with the rationalist exegesis and aimed to elaborate upon their contributions. Instead of affirming or ridiculing the supernatural, Strauss aimed to demonstrate that all Scripture, although not historically factual, are mythological and contain the moral and conceptual truth of Christianity. Aiming to achieve a historical defense of Scriptures only opened Christianity to further criticism, and by moving beyond a historical analysis, one is better able to preserve and understand Christianity's true meaning.

To Strauss, there are three types of myths: the historical, the philosophical, and the poetical. Historical myths are narratives of real events which have later developed mythical presentations, philosophical myths have a clear moral truth behind them, and poetic myths are a combination of both the historical and philosophical—containing some elements of historical truth but developed to reveal a core moral of the story. Therefore, since both the Old and New Testament appear to have some historical basis yet likewise demonstrate signs of the supernatural, they should be classified as poetic myth.

If all Scriptures are mythical, one could question why he gave value to the texts. After all, in the 21st century, the term myth has negative connotations. However, Strauss did not attach a negative connotation to myth. To Strauss, religious myth had value as it represented the spirit of the nation—the *volksgeist*. By taking part in religious practice, the individual expresses the ideals and values of the community that they take part in.[39] Therefore, one can see that Strauss, like Feuerbach, argued that by removing religion's metaphysical assumptions one is able to achieve a more fundamental understanding of humanity.

By presenting religion, especially the Christian faith, as myth, Strauss provides a critical analysis of Christianity which differentiates himself from the supernaturalists and its naturalist critics. While opposed to fundamentalist conceptions of Scripture, it can be argued that Strauss's position is helpful in understanding the possibility of being historically critical of Scriptures without needing to dismiss them entirely. Despite being contrary to the Christian presentation of Scripture, Feuerbach and Strauss provide useful tools for Christians and atheists alike to explore the value of Scripture and its eternal meaning.

Marx, Reductionism, and Religion as the Opium of the People

One of the most influential thinkers of the 19th century, Karl Marx, made great contributions to the socio-economic scene with his ideas of communism, property and religion. However, his radically atheistic stance and highly quotable phrases like "religion… is the opium of the people"[40] make it easy to mischaracterize his arguments. In this section, I will examine Marx's argument that religion was a result of poor socio-economic circumstances and was used as a tool of power to manipulate the weak.

Religion in Marx's Socio-economic Reductionism

Behind Marx's socio-economic reductionism is the

---

39 Frederick C. Beiser, 'The Theory of Myth," *David Friedrich Strauß, Father of Unbelief: An Intellectual Biography* (Oxford, 2020; online edn, Oxford Academic, 22 Oct. 2020), 71.
40 Karl Marx, "Critique of Hegel's Philosophy of Right," in *Marx on Religion,* ed. John C. Raines (Philadelphia: Temple University Press, 2002), 171.

Hegelian notion that history can be understood as a movement of a certain Spirit or Idea through time. However, whereas Hegel presented history as the self-disclosure of Spirit, Marx instead viewed history as the realization of socio-economic movements. Therefore, to Marx, understanding socio-economic movements is the key to understanding everything about the world–religion included.

Based on socio-economic reductionism, Marx proposed that religion was the result of poor socio-economic conditions that humans faced. In face of poor circumstances, humans had to create religion to cope with reality and religion became "the opium of the people."[41] It is clear that Marx is often misunderstood and misinterpreted. As a socio-economic phenomena, Marx did not believe in the intrinsic evil of religion, rather, it was the causes which generated religion that were insidious. Based on the assumption that religion's only purpose was to overcome a poor socio-economic environment, he believed that religion would naturally fade away once the stimuli—a poor environment—was done away with.[42]

Marx's socio-economic reductionism impacts his treatment of religion and separates him from other critics of religion. Unlike atheists who view religion as an expression of false truth claims and therefore aim to challenge Christians based on these truth claims, by stating that religion is the result of socio-economic circumstances instead, Marx would view traditional apologetic dialogue as futile. Rather, Marx makes the bold argument that as long as one resolves the underlying socio-economic problems, the surface level manifestation of religion would self-capitulate.[43] Therefore, Marx would have disagreed with the anti-religious rhetoric provided by the New Atheists and the religious persecution of

---

41 Marx, "Critique of Hegel's Philosophy of Right," in *Marx on Religion,* 171.
42 MacIntyre, *Marxism,* 104.
43 Henri de Lubac, *The Drama of Atheist Humanism,* trans. Edith M. Riley (Cleveland: World Publishing, 1963.), 40.

the 20th century Marxist revolutions. For Marx, such anti-religious polemics and persecutions fundamentally mistake the essence of religion.

Religion in Class Struggle

While Marx did not believe in the intrinsic evil of religion, he did believe that those in power utilized religion as a tool to control those who were suffering. MacIntyre summarizes Marx's position succinctly, "[religion] buttresses the established order by sanctifying it and by suggesting that the political order is somehow ordained by divine authority, and it consoles the oppressed... by offering them in heaven what they are denied on earth."[44] This argument is seen in his treatment of "the Jewish question" where Marx addresses the struggles faced by the Jews. Marx makes the case that the only way to free the Jewish from their struggles was not to change the society around them, but to emancipate them from their Jewish (religious) leanings. Since Judaism, to Marx, embodied the evils of materialism and the desire for physical possessions, he concludes that the "social emancipation of the Jew is the emancipation of society from Judaism."[45] [46] While those in control remain, religious alienation and oppression would remain. Therefore, the only way to free society is to remove the socio-economic structures which uphold the basis of religion.

As such, instead of directly criticizing any tenets of religion, Marx aimed to reduce religion to a socio-economic background. If one were to solve all socio-economic inequalities, religion would naturally disappear. Of course, the application of class struggle to religion was a reiteration of the anti-clerical arguments of the Enlightenment. Nevertheless, Marx should be credited for rekindling these

---

44 MacIntyre, *Marxism*, 103.
45 He writes, "What is the secular cult of the Jew? *Haggling*. What is his secular God? *Money*." (Karl Marx, "On the Jewish Question" in *Marx on Religion,* ed. John C. Raines. (Philadelphia: Temple University Press, 2002), 65)
46 Ibid., 69.

arguments in public awareness and for tying religion to his broader socio-economic analysis.

The Gift of Modernity and a Christian Response

By analyzing the contributions of the 19th century, one can see how prevalent these influences are in modern discussions. In fact, it is surprising to see how little the discussions on secularism have changed over the last two hundred years. By understanding the perspectives of Darwin, Feuerbach, Strauss, or Marx, one is able to understand what is at the heart of many of the arguments that Christians face, helping us respond productively to secular criticism. While each thinker challenges different aspects of religion, they all can be seen as a clash of presuppositions and worldviews, each dictating one's conclusions. By beginning with a study of the human condition, Feuerbach concludes that religion is merely a projection of the human sub-consciousness. By denying the supernatural, Strauss is naturally directed towards a mythical interpretation. Likewise, by viewing history through the lens of socio-economic determinism, Marx concludes that religion is merely the result of poor conditions. Are they wrong? Based on their own set of presuppositions, the answer is no! They have each followed their own methodology to its logical end.

Let us not ignore the fact that even as Christians we often appeal to these 19th century arguments during inter-faith dialogue. Are we not often like Strauss when it comes to discussing the scriptures of other religions? Are we not often like Feuerbach or Marx when we argue that the gods of other religions are fictitious? As modern Christians what separates us from them? Too often, the only difference appears to be our different set of presuppositions. Just as Feuerbach with his anthropology or Marx with his reductionism, Christians take the Bible to be God's word and Christ to be God's one and only Son but we still analyze the world through modern epistemological tools.

Through our analysis of these key contributions in 19th century religious dialogue, a powerful case can be made that during discussions with the secular world, it is not only that we have to address and interact with individual arguments, but also to view these discussions as clashes between worldviews, with interlocutors entering with different presuppositions and assumptions. By recognizing both dimensions of apologetic discourse, one would be more aware of the challenges that are presented, aiding fruitful future dialogue with our secular interlocutors.

MODERN ART–IS IT THAT AWFUL?

Annie Nardone

The Christian is the one whose imagination should fly beyond the stars.

Francis Schaeffer, *Art and the Bible*

I have taught art and humanities courses for many years; in fact, one of my current classes covers the span of 3,000 years of history told through the arts. Typically, when our studies enter the 20th century, the classroom commentary ranges from "that's ugly" to "I don't get it." Occasionally, the comments are less kind, like "I painted like that when I was three," but I caution against categorizing all modern art as ugly before we give it a chance to speak for itself. In his book *Art and the Bible*, Francis Schaeffer wrote that "Modern art often flattens man out and speaks in great abstractions."[1] Often, but not always. There is goodness, truth, and beauty to be found in many pieces created in the 20th and 21st centuries; there is even transcendence, if we give in to curiosity and take time to truly see the magic and the message. To aid your understanding, I have included the name of a significant painting by each artist as an easy reference while you read this essay.

Modern art is often used as a blanket term to cover any recent art, primarily visual pieces, that seem abstract, undefinable, or confusing. However, the true modern art movement is not a 20th century reaction to tradition. Critics and historians debate exactly when modernism began, often crediting Gustave Courbet, a Realist-era artist as the primary influence. Courbet created a sensation in France by painting

---

1 Francis Schaeffer, *Art and the Bible* (Downers Grove: InterVarsity Press, 2006), 90.

the common man in everyday moments, rather than wealthy subjects stiffly posed in elaborate settings. While he may have been controversial in his day for his nudes, hunting, and ordinary landscapes, his claim to notoriety may be weak. Centuries prior to Courbet's work, Rembrandt, Dutch master artist of the 1600s, painted similar images of hunting dogs, dead hares and portraits of street folk centuries before Courbet. Common to both artists is the penchant to paint more introspectively, rather than what was popular in their respective times. Rembrandt refused to imitate the popular classical and dynamic Baroque style, yet still retained the Christian imagery and chiaroscuro technique. Courbet was accused of painting the ugliness of reality and the lower classes in society. Both men pushed against established and valued norms in traditional art circles.

History does not include a proven pivot point where modern art began, but we can observe a slow change in the vision and purpose of what art would represent. Over the centuries, themes in painting and sculpture changed from da Vinci's "The Last Supper" with its visual storytelling embedded with theological symbolism, to Marcel Duchamp's 1917 work "Fountain," the legendary urinal, signed "R. Mutt 1917." Duchamp's creation was displayed in a gallery as a "Readymade"—the term to describe "an ordinary manufactured object designated by the artist as a work of art."[2] Biblical themes faded into history as secular statement pieces came to the forefront.

Society, especially as it relates to the field of art, has moved from a desire for transcendent meaning to shifting relativism and from visual narrative to abstraction. Why is it that we have a visceral reaction when looking at modern art? Is it because it is fragmented and without meaning? The slow progression over the past 400+ years of human creativity

---

2 Tate Museum U.K., Marcel Duchamp "Fountain" 1917, March 18, 2024. https://www.tate.org.uk/art/artworks/duchamp-fountain-t07573.

shows us the important influences that set us on our pathway to modern art. The work of the pre-Renaissance artist's vision demonstrated an outward purpose of religious revelation, piety, and reverence, which eventually changed to the 20th century's inward purpose of the modern artist's desire to focus on his or her personal statement and values. Historically, art and image-making reflected goodness, truth, beauty, and storymaking. The past century has revealed a shift to art for the sake of social commentary, with obtuse images of themes, media, and techniques representing individual meaning or as a protest piece for the artist. Does that render the art unrelatable or not even worth pondering? Why should we bother to try and understand?

For the purpose of exploration of the modern movement, we need to examine painting and sculpture, as well as the newer media of photography. In *Visual Faith*, William A. Dyrness writes, "Culture has made a turn toward the visual, and with the rise of new media, the visual image has come to occupy an unprecedented central place in our lives."[3] We should consider the modern importance placed on the visual "hit," where the viewer is shocked into attention, versus a more cerebral approach where the reader is drawn into the classical piece to ponder its complexity, symbolism, color, and design elements. There can be merit in modern art; for example, some pieces tap into the techniques of the old masters during the time of the Renaissance. Stratford Caldecott dedicates entire chapters in his book, *Beauty for Truth's Sake—On the Re-enchantment of Education*, to the mathematics and symbolism of the sacred numbers, irrational beauty, Fibonacci sequence, and golden ratios. Artists and architects have incorporated these principles into their work for centuries, creating visual stability. Those ancient design practices can be found in modern art as well. Caldecott writes, "Both Leonardo da Vinci and Piet Mondrian

---

3 William A. Dyrness, *Visual Faith-Art, Theology, and Worship in Dialogue* (Grand Rapids: Baker Academic, 2001), 156.

used such rectangles frequently in their paintings, and the [golden] ratio itself can be found governing the lengths of sections in many Beethoven movements."[4] At first glance, Mondrian's painting *Broadway Boogie Woogie* (1943) looks like an assemblage of colored squares, but the artist used golden ratios to create a visually pleasing exploration of line and color.

Because our lives are inundated with images that challenge our senses and comprehension, we are inclined to dismiss any urge to study modern art. Viewing Pablo Picasso's distortions and Jackson Pollock's paint splatters challenges our imaginations. But understanding the purposeful design and motivation in modern art is worth the study. Some suggest that there has been a devolution in art in the 20th century. Certainly, signed urinals [*Fountain*, Duchamp (1917)] and geometric figures centered on the science of motion [*Nude Descending a Staircase*, Duchamp (1912)] were created to challenge our understanding of the purpose of creativity or even what defines an object as art. Dadaists, who included avant-garde artist Duchamp and photographer Man Ray, reacted against WWI and used art as objects of protest against cultural norms and traditions, challenging society to define art.

Do we feel ill at ease with modern art because it appears fractured, outside of creation, and irrational? There are many factors to consider before a quick judgment is made, for instance: subject, balance, color, line, texture, space/mass/volume, perspective, proportion, the influence of the sacred numbers, Golden Mean, Phi, and the Fibonacci sequence. Modern art explores the intersection of composition, color, and shape, so we can find beauty even in some abstract art because it was purposely designed. The paintings of Paul Klee [*Twittering Machine* (1922) and *Ships in*

---

4 Stratford Caldecott, *Beauty for Truth's Sake-On the Re-enchantment of Education*. (Grand Rapids: Brazos Press, 2009), 67.

the Dark (1927)] appear cartoonish and random. Then you discover that "Klee was a natural draftsman who experimented with and eventually deeply explored color theory, writing about it extensively; his lectures *Writings on Form and Design Theory*, published as the *Paul Klee Notebooks*, are held to be as important for modern art as Leonardo da Vinci's *A Treatise on Painting* was for the Renaissance."[5]

Modern art has largely become a statement on culture or what is happening in society. The themes and images have morphed from expression and reverence and looking toward a creator to art that is meaningful only to the artist. Focus has shifted to how the artist feels, disregarding how other people are affected when looking at the piece. Many times, it's all about "me, the artist", not the Creator who inspires and who created us in His image, giving us the joy of co-creating as an act of worship. Art can be used as a political statement or social commentary, or perhaps spur society on to change. 20th century non-representational art is not only image driven; it is also theory driven and experimental, moody or playful, and challenging to comprehend.

Modern art was created as a reaction to the times in which the artists lived: the cruelty and suffering of WWI, The Dust Bowl and Depression, atomic war, industrialization, the worldwide rise of dictatorships, commercialism and loss of identity of the 1960s, and the secularization of societies once grounded in faith. The canvas was their sounding board where they expressed frustration with the status quo of art and society. And as those secular voices rose, the voice of the church that knew beauty and wonder stepped back into the shadows, removing itself from the cultural conversation instead of actively engaging with the progression of the arts. Christians find themselves poorly equipped to engage in the

---

5 "Paul Klee", Tate Museum, accessed February 28, 2024. https://www.tate.org.uk/art/artists/paul-klee-1417#:~:text=Klee%20was%20a%20natural%20draftsman,for%20modern%20art%20as%20Leonardo.

present conversation because they cut themselves out of over 100 years of the cultural arts movement. We do not frequent museums or value the visual arts, nor do we challenge younger generations to study the humanities and eras throughout history. John Skillen, author of Putting Art (back) In Its Place, writes, "Most of us remain poorly equipped by our own cultural training to seek out, or even to expect, let alone to understand, the relationships once at work between artworks and their architectural, liturgical, and narrative settings."[6] If we cannot speak the same language as the creators, we cannot understand what they create. The Christian voice has become culturally moot.

But I consider this a pause, not an end. Christian artists are once again engaging in the community of makers, not creating as had always been done, but with surprising abstractions and deeper meaning. Josh Tiessen[7] makes his mark in Christian art by returning to the symbolism and hyper-surrealism, inspired by his definition of the "holy weirdness" in scripture and the works of medieval painter Hieronymous Bosch [*The Last Judgment,* (1482) and *The Garden of Earthly Delights*, (1515)]. Tiessen wrote, "In my escapades through art history, I've found many artists of faith who have integrated the wild and wonderful in their work. Perhaps we can look to them as guides, or at least conversational partners as we aim to reconcile an ancient faith with a postmodern world."[8] God spoke creation into existence. He spoke in representations of goodness, truth and beauty, not religious art. We live in His divine, three-dimensional masterpiece. A Christian artist does not need to concentrate on religious subjects to convey sacred meaning.

There are modern artists who embrace the abstract, a

---

6 John Skillen, *Putting Art (back) In Its Place* (Peabody: Hendrickson Publishers, 2016), 219.
7 If you would like to learn more about Tiessen's inspiring life, art, and exhibitions, please visit his website: https://www.joshtiessen.com/.
8 Josh Tiessen, "A Call for Weird Christian Art," *Ekstasis Magazine*, February 2024. https://ekstasismagazine.substack.com/p/a-call-for-weird-christian-art.

peculiar kind of illustration, using unusual and rare materials as a reflection of the priceless design that our Creator used in creating us.

Makoto Fujimura, founder of the International Arts Movement, Fujimura Institute, and co-founder of the Kintsugi Academy, has been connecting his Christian faith with modern arts culture for over thirty years. I encourage you to study his paintings, especially his *Four Holy Gospels*.[9] Mako approaches his work as a spiritual necessity, connecting with God's inspiration to create pieces that reflect the intersection between awe and wonder with scripture and nature. He believes that "artists are the conduits of life, articulating what all of us are surely sensing but may not have the capacity to express."[10] The act of making guides us into a richer understanding of God's grace, mercy, and love as we become co-creators with Him here on earth.

How do you begin to understand the complexity of modern art? Find a museum with galleries displaying the work of modern masters, including Salvador Dali's Surrealism [*The Persistence of Memory*] and Jackson Pollock's immense canvases of splattered and streaked color and dimensional texture. You will gain a deeper appreciation of the artist's media technique and the subtle touches in color and brushstroke. Pollock's work is an expressive deep dive into emotion and color. Ask the docents for interesting facts. Oftentimes, they share obscure insights! I stood in front of Pollock's *Number 1 (Lavender Mist)* (1950) at the National Gallery of Art, Washington DC, and asked the docent what he thought of the painting. He smiled and pointed out a burnt cigarette and raisin stuck in the paint and an unfortunate cockroach that had plowed itself into the wet media to become

---

9 Makoto Fujimura, *Four Holy Gospels*, historic commission of paintings rendered as illuminations commemorating the 400th anniversary of the *King James Bible*, 2011. https://makotofujimura.com/art/portals/four-holy-gospels.

10 Makoto Fujimura, *Art + Faith* (Yale: Yale University Press, 2020), 107.

part of the work. At that moment, Pollock's studio became a real place to me.

Is all modern art ugly and unredeemable? Certainly not. There is order in what first appears to be chaos. Modern art explores the intersection of composition, color, and shape to make even abstract art feel as if it makes sense. On the other hand, during a visit to the Museum of Modern Art at the NGA, my young daughter walked up to a large metal box surrounded by perforated metal and tossed in her candy wrapper. In her defense, the sculpture looked like a trash can. Some art demands a herculean effort to understand and appreciate.

What does modern art ask of us? Patience. Curiosity. A sense of wonder about the artist's voice and what is expressed in the work. Christians must find a way to integrate back into the art scene—not taking over, but reestablishing our place in the creative conversation. A helpful step to that end is to familiarize yourself with what feels like strange territory. The bibliography of this essay will provide texts to help you navigate through the ideas shared here. We need not be intimidated by the modern art movement.

> *May we steward well what the Creator King has given us, and accept God's invitation to sanctify our imagination and creativity, even as we labor hard on this side of eternity. May our art, what we make, be multiplied into the New Creation.*
>
> – Makoto Fujimura, "A Benediction for Makers," *Art + Faith*

Article Bibliography

Fujimura, Makoto. *Art + Faith*. Yale: Yale University Press, 2020.

Dyrness, William A. *Visual Faith-Art, Theology, and Worship in Dialogue*. Grand Rapids: Baker Academic, 2001.

Schaeffer, Francis. *Art and the Bible*. Downers Grove: InterVarsity Press, with revisions by L'Abri Fellowship, 2006.

Caldecott, Stratford. *Beauty for Truth's Sake-On the Re-enchantment of Education*. Grand Rapids: Brazos Press, 2009.

Skillen, John. *Putting Art (back) in its Place*. Peabody, MA: Hendrickson Publishers, 2016.

Saccardi, Marianne. *Art in Story: Teaching Art to Elementary School Children.* Westport, CT: Greenwood Publishing Group, 2007.

Glaspey, Terry. *75 Masterpieces Every Christian Should Know*. Grand Rapids: Baker Books, 2015

Hamlet
and the Headless World

Annie Crawford

Shakespearean critic E.M.W. Tillyard described the tragedy of *Hamlet* as "one of the most medieval as well as one of the most acutely modern of Shakespeare's plays."[1] As the Scientific Revolution, the Protestant Reformation, and the humanistic Renaissance triggered the cultural shifts that birthed the modern era, Shakespeare placed his inky-cloaked, brooding Prince on the precipice of the brave new modern world. The well-ordered theistic cosmos that shaped the medieval imagination was beginning to be dismantled and replaced by the modern perspective wherein man and not God was the new measure of all things. The foundation for knowledge and authority in Western culture was slowly shifting from the transcendent to the material until, at last, Darwin's theory of natural selection fully inaugurated the change of regime. Once the miracle of life became fully explicable through material causality alone, the 'God hypothesis' seemed no longer necessary and the rational mind of man appeared to be the zenith of being, the lone crown of the cosmos. So now, like Hamlet four hundred years before, we find ourselves living within the cosmic court of an illegitimate king, for man was not created to be an authority unto himself. We too are Claudius, Gertrude, and the treasonous court of a God-haunted kingdom. Thus, through the motif of regicide developed in the tragedy of *Hamlet*, Shakespeare provides us a prophetic vision of our modern atheistic world. Neither a kingdom that condones the reign of

---

1 Quoted in Joseph Pearce, introduction to *Hamlet* by William Shakespeare, Ignatius Critical Edition, ed. Joseph Pearce (San Francisco: Ignatius Press, 2008), xii.

the murderous usurper Claudius nor a culture that rejects God as the source of authority will any longer be able to justify morality, discern the truth, or perceive the meaning of beauty.

Sick with corruption, uncertainty, and anxiety, the rotten state of Denmark offers a clear window into the nature of the modern, godless cosmos, for regicide is a rejection of the transcendent moral authority through which any just government rules. As King David knew, to kill the Lord's anointed is to reject the anointing of the Lord. When the rightful king is murdered, the ordering center of the kingdom is shattered. Thus, after the treacherous murder of King Hamlet, Shakespeare shows all of Denmark cast "out of joint."[2] Horatio compares the events in Denmark to the unnatural disasters which befell Rome after Julius Caesar was murdered. As the head was treacherously cut off from the body politic, the "sheeted dead / Did squeak and gibber in the Roman streets," and the heavens forebode disaster through falling stars—"disasters in the sun" and a moon "Sick almost to doomsday with eclipse."[3] As in Rome, so too disaster looms in Denmark as the false king begins his reign under threat of war yet "with mirth in funeral, and with dirge in marriage."[4] The guards have become "sick at heart" and a ghost haunts the castle gate.[5] One man's will to power has abolished the source of legitimate authority and turned the entire kingdom upside down. Shakespearian scholar Joseph Pierce argues that Hamlet was not "a madman but... a man maddened by the moral madness that surrounds him."[6] Denmark's acceptance of the usurper and the maintenance of business-as-usual were the true lunacy.

Like Claudius, moderns too have murdered the true King and thrust the whole of our Western kingdom into chaos. It

---

[2] William Shakespeare, *Hamlet,* Ignatius Critical Edition, ed. By Joseph Pearce (San Francisco: Ignatius Press, 2008), 1.5.189.
[3] Shakespeare, *Hamlet,* 1.1.115-120.
[4] Shakespeare, *Hamlet,* 1.2.12.
[5] Ibid., 1.1.8.
[6] Pearce, introduction, xxv.

was Charles Darwin's final rejection of teleology that enabled Nietzsche to announce the death of God, though it had "not yet reached the ears of men," for "deeds, though done, still require time to be seen and heard."[7] Yet Darwin's denial of purposeful design within the material realm was in essence a denial of the ordering rule and presence of God. Before Darwin wrote his *On the Origin of the Species*, design had been the default paradigm for understanding the world. For example, Cicero wondered, "which is there among [things celestial and things terrestrial] which does not clearly display the rational design of an intelligent being?"[8] In his *Autobiography*, Darwin admitted to "the extreme difficulty or rather impossibility of conceiving this immense and wonderful universe... as the result of blind chance or necessity. When thus reflecting I feel compelled to look to a First Cause... and I deserve to be called a Theist."[9] However, the "very old argument from the existence of suffering against the existence of an intelligent First Cause" seemed compelling to Darwin, and he believed he had found an alternative to special creation in the theory of natural selection.[10] If Darwin was correct, then all the *apparent* design, intelligence, and beauty we encounter in the material world is not in fact a meaningful manifestation of the Creator's wisdom but merely the fortuitous result of impersonal, blind processes. Darwin believed that "the old argument from design in Nature, as given by Paley, which formerly seemed to me so conclusive, fails, now that the law of natural selection has been discovered."[11] In that last stronghold of the old kingdom, Biology, the Creator was removed. Life had been the

---

7 Friedrich Nietzsche, *The Joyful Wisdom*, trans. Thomas Common (1924), Book 5, No. 343, in the eBooks@Adelaide digital library, accessed February 18, 2018, https://ebooks.adelaide.edu.au/n/nietzsche/friedrich/n67j/book5.html.
8 Cicero, On the Nature of the Gods, II.XXXVII.
9 Charles Darwin, *Autobiography,* in The Portable Atheist: Essential Readings for the Nonbeliever, ed. Christopher Hitchens (Philadelphia: Da Capo Press, 2007), 96.
10 Ibid., 95.
11 Ibid., 94.

last physical reality resisting a mere material explanation. But now that the theory of natural selection seemed to rebuff the possibility of perceiving divine action anywhere at all, Nietzsche astutely concluded that "belief in the Christian God has become unworthy of belief."[12] The King is dead, and as Nietzsche told us, "We have killed him—you and I. All of us are his murderers."[13]

When a culture denies the transcendent source and ground of all being, the ordering principle which holds reality together, it will lose its grasp on the qualities of being, namely goodness, truth, and beauty. Let us first consider goodness. In the pre-modern world, goodness was defined by our ability to fulfill divine purposes—what Aristotle called the *telos* or end goal of things. Darwin's denial of teleological, or purposeful, design destroyed the classical meaning of goodness, for without reference to a Divine Creator, objective purposes and values cannot exist. If the cosmos is designed by a good creator for certain purposes, then goodness can be defined by the fulfillment of those objective purposes. If a watch is made to tell time, then a *good* watch will be one which fulfills this purpose by accurately keeping time, and a *bad* watch will be one which does not fulfill its purpose to tell time. Likewise, if God created man to be the image of God, then a *good* man will be one who reflects the character of God and a *bad* man will be one who does not. However, Darwin's substitution of blind forces for God's purposeful action has removed the concepts of purpose and design from our understanding of the biological world. Consequently, a being's goodness can no longer be defined according to a being's design. Without the reality of a purposeful design, there can no longer be a meaningful distinction between that which is and that which ought to be.

Such is the court of Claudius who in killing the King for his own personal gain denied the design and purpose of the

---

12 Nietzsche, *The Joyful Wisdom*, Book 5, No. 343.
13 Nietzsche, *The Joyful Wisdom*, Book 5, No. 343.

crown and thereby destroyed the moral stability of the kingdom. There can be no goodness in a government founded on treachery. A king's right to rule can only be established by the objective existence of an outside authority. This is why David refused to kill King Saul. David understood that he could not become the legitimate king of a stable kingdom through murder, for if he could slay the Lord's anointed, what would there be to prevent another man from slaying him? We can only form a coherent and peaceful social order when we are all ruled by something higher than ourselves that unites us. When Denmark is overtaken by a murderous usurper such as Claudius, all moral order and the possibility of legitimate authority is undermined, for the kingdom is now united not by loyalty to a higher principle but only by the selfish will of Claudius. Without lawful succession to the throne, the right to rule becomes merely a question of the will to power, and a kingdom created by the personal will to power can only lead to endless violence and the inevitable destruction of the social order. In the court of Claudius, political authority is no longer derived from the moral center of a rightly ordered cosmos; thus, behavior in the kingdom is no longer regulated by adherence to a transcendent Good but rather by compliance to the selfish desires of a tyrant. Thus, in Denmark one can smile and yet be a villain.[14]

This is the moral tragedy ensnaring Rosencrantz and Guildenstern, who are called in to faithfully serve the king yet by that obedience are forced into betrayal. For Rosencrantz and Guildenstern, as for all the subjects of Denmark, to obey the false King is to participate in his tyranny and injustice. Those who, like Prince Hamlet, remain loyal to the Good are put into inevitable conflict with the tyrant. Thus, tyrants always create such fractured, sick societies for there will always be faithful men who love the Good more than power.

In order to support the pretense of Claudius's right to the throne—which ought to have been handed in lawful

---

14 Shakespeare, *Hamlet*, 1.5.108.

succession to the king's son, the young Hamlet—the entire court is drawn into this world of deceit. Moral corruption can only ever sustain itself through lies, for the true and the good are inseparable. Evil always involves a distortion of truth, for evil action itself implicitly claims that harm is a good. Living in the Gulags, Alexandr Solzhenitsyn learned that "violence does not live alone and is not capable of living alone. It is necessarily interwoven with falsehood. Between them lies the most intimate, the deepest of natural bonds. Violence finds its only refuge in falsehood, falsehood its only support in violence. Any man who has once acclaimed violence as his METHOD must inexorably choose falsehood as his PRINCIPLE."[15] Such a man is Caudius, who having obtained the crown by violence must now rule by deceit. The language of the court has been uprooted from reality and put in the service of Claudius's lie. The king's speeches are full of contradictions, distortions, and equivocations. He chides Hamlet's grief as "unmanly" and showing "a will most incorrect to heaven," "A fault to heaven / A fault against the dead, a fault against nature," when in truth Hamlet is the only one still interested in the will of heaven or faults against the dead. Polonius would convince Ophelia that Hamlet's love is mere show, and Rosencrantz and Guildenstern come as friends turned to spies. Denmark has become a kingdom where "words fly up [but] thoughts remain below."[16] Because Claudius cannot speak the truth to his people without giving up his false crown, the dialogue of Denmark has become like Derrida's "outsideless" language.[17] Words in the Danish court no longer point toward a true reality but instead have become mere vehicles for political posturing.

The breakdown of language in the court of Elsinore

---

15 Alexandr Solzhenitsyn, "Nobel Lecture" (1970), NobelPrize.org, accessed 12 Apr 2024, https://www.nobelprize.org/prizes/literature/1970/solzhenitsyn/lecture/.
16 Shakespeare, *Hamlet*, 3.4.97.
17 Malcolm Guite, Faith, Hope, and Poetry: Theology and the Poetic Imagination (London: Routledge, 2016), 8.

mirrors the breakdown of language in our post-truth world where words no longer serve as a medium through which we access an objective, knowable reality. Cut off from its foundation in the Divine *Logos*, truth in an atheistic world can no longer be known with certainty, for we no longer have a real, stable truth to which words can refer. Rather, as the poet Malcom Guite explains, in the postmodern conception of language "every decoding is another encoding;" thus, "supposedly meaning-laden language is reduced to ultimate meaninglessness."[18] The general rejection of theism severs language from truth and now, like Hamlet, we seem to merely play with "words, words, words."[19] The linguistic world of the materialist—a world formed only by self-referential externals—has no real meaning. The material things we see, the things which show, have no meaning unless they are connected to spiritual realities, to an objective correlative that stands outside the physical realm. Things can only mean something in relation to something else. The material realm itself cannot be meaningful unless it exists in relation to another realm that can provide a stable reference point.

Thirdly, for both the grieving Prince Hamlet and the atheistic modern, the loss of goodness and truth reduces beauty to no more than an illusion. For the medieval theist, beauty was "truth shining into being" and the glory of God beckoning the human heart toward communion with the transcendent.[20] However, the denial of teleology and God's meaningful presence in the world entails that our sense of the beauty in nature is no more than a neurological phenomenon or a mere artifice of fancy. As Darwin explained, the rejection of the design argument means "we can no longer argue that, for instance, the beautiful hinge of a bivalve shell must have been made by an intelligent being, like the hinge of a door by

---

18 Ibid., 9.
19 Shakespeare, *Hamlet*, 2.2.191.
20 Quoted in Luci Shaw, "Beauty and the Creative Impulse," in *The Christian Imagination: The Practice of Faith in Literature and Writing*, ed., Leland Ryken (Colorado Springs: Waterbrook Press, 2011), 82, Digital edition.

man. There seems to be no more design in the variability of organic beings... than in the course which the wind blows."[21] Darwin might have quoted directly from Hamlet in order to express the way in which purposelessness transforms beauty to an illusion, to the mere "quintessence of dust."[22] Without a transcendent source of beauty, there is no more reason to call a bivalve shell beautiful than there is a sewage drain. Without the presence of the King to infuse nature with his glory, Hamlet rightly sees that "this most excellent canopy the air... this brave o'erhanging firmament, this majestical roof fretted with golden fire—why it appeareth no other thing to me than a foul and pestilent congregation of vapors."[23] While Darwin began his life as a theist who experienced a sense of the transcendent through the beauty of nature, in later years he confessed that "the grandest scenes would not [now] cause any such conviction and feelings to arise in my mind. It may be truly said that I am like a man who has become colour-blind."[24]

Like Darwin, moderns now trod the earth with eyes blinded to the handiwork of God. Our inability to perceive the transcendental qualities of goodness, truth, and beauty inherent in the material world has rendered our society increasingly immoral, incoherent, and ugly. Without transcendent significance or inherent goodness, the beauty of this world cannot mean anything more than that which happens to stimulate pleasure in the observer. In a purposeless world, there is no objective reason why symmetry, harmony, or balance should be any more objectively beautiful than discord, asymmetry, or brute simplicity. As the Marquis de Sade understood, in a godless world even deriving pleasure from cruelty is perfectly rational and permissible.

Yet modernity, like Claudius, must reach the end of its

---

21 Darwin, *Autobiography*, 94.
22 Shakespeare, *Hamlet*, 2.2.307.
23 Shakespeare, *Hamlet*, 2.2.299-303.
24 Darwin, *Autobiography*, 95-96.

reign. The absurdity and insipidity inherent to tyrannical rule will eventually bring about its own collapse. Although the aged kingdom is sick with conflict and deceit, it is not truly void of meaning. Like the ghost of King Hamlet, real goodness, truth, and beauty cannot truly die. The world is not a vacuum in which we can construct a fresh, clean reality that will suit and serve our selfish ambition. God has embedded transcendent values and meanings into the whole of his creation. Like our own immortal soul, the meaning of things can be twisted and damaged—we can damn them—but we cannot exterminate them. Neither Claudius, nor Darwin, nor we can escape that which truly *is.* The King—the source of all goodness, truth, and beauty who is the foundation of a just and flourishing culture—still and always reigns. As Hamlet came to understand, even in a world that seems turned upside down, there is yet "special providence in the fall of a sparrow."[25] Though all the world kiss the tyrant, still we with Hamlet can choose the right. "The readiness is all."[26]

---

25 Shakespeare, *Hamlet,* 5.2.211-212.
26 Ibid., 5.2.215.

AFTER THE LIGHT

James M. Swayze

This poem is a reflection on knowledge (light, vision), rebellion, and forgetting. It directly refers to the first two lines of George Herbert's "Love (III)" and indirectly to the first three lines that open Milton's "Paradise Lost." With a brief nod to ancient Greece, it traces the West's simultaneous ascent and descent—from the Enlightenment, when our eyes were 'opened' and, blinded by our own brilliance, we began to lose sight of our Creator; to Modernism's meaninglessness, at which point we'd forgotten about God altogether (wondering whether he'd ever existed in the first place); to the vacuity of Postmodernism and our faith in nothing at all, save some vague, undefinable "progress."

After the Light

Love bids us welcome, ever.
We hear its thunder, briefly apprehend,
But in a lightning-flash forget.
Resigned to obscurity,
We sightlessly stumble, high road to low.

Long ago, nearly too long to remember,
The new seer comforted those who would seek.
We were newly-crowned possessors of the golden
    polis.

Somehow discontent, though well-supplied,
Of late, we chose to re-draw the well-drawn map
So there now seems no longer a city to seek,
No guilt, no dust, no sin, no light.

By our own lights, we were freed but emptied,
    enlightened but alone.
Yet in that rare stillness, we could not, we cannot
    shake the nagging suspicion
That what used to be still could be, still *is*.
And while thinking will not make it so, neither will
    feeling.
And our final resort, wishing, will not make it go
    away.

Yes, once there was a way,
Now butchered by the punch-clock, the madmen,
A way practiced by simple men in simple times,
Simpletons who could not know what now we
    know.

Ever onward and upward moving,
Enlightened man turned to doubting man, doubting
    first his creator's intentions,
Then his capacity, then whether he'd even answer
    the door,
Doubted then the door itself.

In now slips the even-newer knower.
He is a man of two minds,[1] knowing
That in the past all men said 'knowing', but meant
    by it only to show
How the well-lit path leads to an empty lot
And mean words to an end.

---

1 See James 1:8

Grasping the newly-vacant scepter, this Super-Man
    to be,
His promises empty, will enslave as he would free.

Plucking the unripe fruit from the tree,
He dissects, consumes, regurgitates,
Leaving at his feet malumic[2] remains.

Where once our souls drew back, convicted of sin
Now we draw back only transparent skin.

---

2 A neologism, from the Latin *malum*, "apple."

Freeing Michelangelo's Prisoners

By Jasmin Biggs

Michelangelo's Prisoners changed me. In the final year of my undergraduate degree, I had the privilege of studying abroad in Italy for three weeks. At the Galleria dell'Accademia museum in Florence, Michelangelo's *David* was as exquisite as I expected. But I was not prepared for my profound encounter with his unfinished works. The forms of four human bodies are trapped in raw stone, dynamically striving with all their energy to shake themselves free.[1]

In beholding them, I glimpsed a parable writ large. These powerful forms seek order out of chaos, truth out of nonsense, identity out of facelessness. Yet they are imprisoned. They are only in process, not completed. They are a picture of what it means to be human. Humans are born into subjectivity, striving for objectivity. We are ever becoming in our journey towards truth and wholeness.

To me, these statues represent where the best of modernism and the best of postmodernism meet. Few Christians study postmodernism. The few who do typically seek to refute it. My own understanding only scratches the surface. But in my study, I have noticed that postmodern thought does emphasize an indispensable principle, subjectivity, that we cannot neglect if our goal is to uncover the objective truth that modernism promises. I believe that Christians need the best of postmodernism to accomplish the goal of modernism: objective truth.

For the sake of this piece, I am using the terms

---

1 Michaelangelo, "Michelangelo's Prisoners (or Slaves)," *AccademiaGallery.Org*. Last modified November 2, 2023, accessed April 13, 2024, https://accademiagallery.org/michelangelos-prisoners-or-slaves/.

"modernism" and "postmodernism" as shorthand for broad epistemological (knowledge-seeking) postures. In simplified terms, modernism refers to the position, popular during the Enlightenment, that pure logic and evidence are sufficient for attaining objective truth. Meanwhile, postmodernism refers to the position that there is no objective truth that humans can access; instead, the best we have is subjective, individual "truths" or perspectives. Neither are fully correct. Yet both offer some key insights we ought to consider. Of course, modernism and postmodernism are huge movements, spanning hundreds of years and encompassing many camps and shades of meaning. But these definitions will suffice for today's discussion.

Natural Revelation

The foundation for today's discussion is the biblical principle of natural revelation. While I affirm the unique role of God's special revelation in Scripture, the Bible itself teaches that God does not exclusively communicate knowledge through Scripture. He tells us in Psalm 19, "The heavens declare the glory of God, and the skies proclaim his handiwork. Day after day they pour forth speech; night after night they display *knowledge*. There is no speech or language where their voice is not heard. Their voice goes out into all the earth; their words to the ends of the world."[2] According to this passage, God does not only reveal knowledge through Scripture. He also uses the natural world to reveal knowledge—a world rich in data, color, and the diversity of human experience.

As this Psalm tells us, it is not only in one language or one culture where God reveals truth. Scripture reiterates this principle in Acts 17, where Paul preaches to the pagan Athenians on Mars Hill to affirm and build upon the natural revelation they had received. He even affirms the truth

---

2 Psalm 19:1-2 (NET), emphasis added.

discovered by their pagan poets: "As even some of your own poets have said, 'For we too are [God's] offspring'."[3] Similarly, Romans 1 clearly states that God reveals himself to all people: "What can be known about God is plain to them, because God has made it plain to them. For since the creation of the world his invisible attributes—his eternal power and divine nature—have been clearly seen, because they are understood through what has been made… "[4] God created every human being with the *Imago Dei* (the Image of God), so every human being has access to some amount of knowledge and truth through natural revelation. While natural revelation is evident, for instance, through Western culture, it is also evident through other cultures and people groups. God can reveal truth through natural revelation in every language, in every era, in every culture, to every image bearer, throughout the whole world.

God reserves the right to communicate with us however he pleases, including through natural means. It is his divine prerogative to reveal knowledge this way. And since God reveals certain truths about himself to every culture and language, that would include the modern and postmodern eras. So we must not mistakenly assume that God stopped revealing himself once the modern era began. Natural revelation did not screech to a halt. God continues to reveal himself through the testimony of modern image-bearers, the story of history, the insights and experiences of the global church, and the discoveries of scholarship. Wherever God reveals truth, we should listen.

This may seem too obvious to be stated. Unfortunately, some extreme yet influential figures, such as Doug Wilson and Joe Rigney, are actively teaching that empathy itself is a sin.[5]

---

3 Acts 17:28b (NET).
4 Romans 1:19b-20a (NET).
5 Joseph Rigney, "The Enticing Sin of Empathy," *Desiring God*, May 31, 2019, accessed April 13, 2024, https://www.desiringgod.org/articles/the-enticing-sin-of-empathy. See also the YouTube conversation titled "The Sin of Empathy | Doug Wilson and Joe Rigney," published by *YouTube channel Canon Press*,

Furthermore, they teach that the observations and insights of whole groups of Christian believers, such as women, are dangerous to the life of the church and should be disregarded out of hand.[6] Hence, it is necessary to explicitly present an apologetic for the value of natural revelation wherever—and through whomever—God chooses to reveal it. In a similar vein, many Christians may feel threatened by "the culture," defined as the secular world outside of Christian subculture. Many may struggle to imagine that modernism or postmodernism have anything of value to offer to our faith. So it is worth taking the time to understand how God reveals certain tenets of knowledge even through modernism and postmodernism.

Many Christians study such movements simply to refute them and justify what they already believe. But we would not want an atheist to study Christianity in this way, reading our Scripture, our apologists, and our philosophers only to critique, refute, and dismiss. "Do unto others" applies also to how we study. The goal is to seek truth as objectively as we can, even if that means revising our own views. The endeavor of cultural analysis takes humility and open-mindedness, seeking to allow the data to correct and shape the raw stone of our preexisting biases.

The Role of Imagination

One major (and perhaps surprising) problem with modernity's project of seeking objective truth is that it historically neglected the role of imagination. When we think of imagination, we may picture dragons, superheroes, and general nerdery. But imagination is in fact crucial not only for the shape of our words, but also for the shape of our thinking. Imagination is a crucial building block for all of thought,

---

https://www.youtube.com/watch?v=6i9a3Rfd7yI&ab_channel=CanonPress.
6 Joseph Rigney, "Empathy, Feminism, and the Church," *American Reformer*, January 26, 2024, accessed April 13, 2024,
https://americanreformer.org/2024/01/empathy-feminism-and-the-church/.

language, and communication. C.S. Lewis explains that "Reason is the natural organ of truth; but imagination is the organ of meaning."[7] In other words, imagination is the mental faculty that gives content, or meaning, to the words and concepts we reason *about*. What do we picture when we hear certain words, like "father," "church," "career," "welfare," or "woke?" Do those pictures have positive or negative connotations? Are we sure we have the whole picture, and that that picture is accurate? When Lewis tells us that imagination is the organ of meaning, he is pointing out that logic is not enough. We must also carefully consider whether we understand the *meanings* behind the terms that we use.

But imagination does more than give meaning to the words we use. It also largely defines what data about reality we *notice*. English professor and cultural critic Karen Swallow Prior offers some crucial insights on this in her book *Evangelical Imagination*. She explains, "While the objective world in all its entirety exists all around us, our imagination draws only from what we perceive. And we primarily perceive what we attend to."[8] In other words, we think about what we notice. So it is worth interrogating what data we notice, and perhaps even more importantly, what data we do not notice.

We all have the same objective world, in all its entirety, around us. We swim in an ocean of data. And with that data are countless observations and endless interpretations of what that data *means*—what reality is *really* like. So how is it that one data set produces liberals and conservatives, fundamentalists and environmentalists, traditionalists and postmodernists, Christians and atheists, Hindus and Muslims, libertarians, communists, and fascists? How do we all come to such dramatically different conclusions about the nature of reality?

---

7 C.S. Lewis, "Bluspels and Flalansferes: A Semantic Nightmare," in *Selected Literary Essays* (Cambridge: Cambridge University Press, 2018), 265.
8 Karen Swallow Prior, *The Evangelical Imagination* (Grand Rapids: Brazos Press, 2023), 12.

A big part of the answer is that we imagine the world differently. The fact is that we are born into a tiny portion of the full data set. All of us are born naked and ignorant; no one is born omniscient. To fill in the gaps, each of us uses our imagination to construct a picture of what the rest of reality is like. Throughout our upbringing, we are taught how to imagine the world by parents, teachers, books, and stories, which all themselves come from various persuasions. But each of us only has firsthand knowledge of a small portion of the total dataset.

There is no shame in ignorance per se. We have each had a limited number of years on this earth, with limited life experience and limited time to think about the endlessly varied questions of theology, philosophy, and life. We are finite. Only God is infinite. So our knowledge is finite. We are inevitably ignorant of the totality of the data about reality.

So we must make peace with our ignorance as a necessary condition of being born. We must enter the world not as a know-it-all but as an eager-to-know-more. Admitting that we don't know something is vastly superior to pretending we know everything. Even the wisest person will always be open to more information, to a deeper understanding.

Paul himself, an author of Scripture, admits to incomplete, imperfect knowledge. He remarks that "we know in part, and we prophesy in part, but when what is perfect comes, the partial will be set aside... now we see in a mirror indirectly, but then we will see face to face. Now I know in part, but then I will know fully, just as I have been fully known."[9] How many of us could claim to know as much as Paul about theology? Yet even Paul admits to partial knowledge, imperfection, and seeing darkly.

So we tend to notice data about the world that conforms with how we already imagine the world to be. Another name for this is confirmation bias. In his book *When Doctrine Divides the People of God*, theologian Rhyne Putman studies how

---

9 1 Corinthians 13:9-10, 12 (NET).

confirmation bias affects biblical interpretation. He defines it as "the way someone unwittingly uses and selects evidence that confirms his or her previously held belief or working hypothesis."[10] What we perceive, and what we pay attention to, is often limited by the imaginary picture of the world we want to confirm. So we each pay attention to different pieces of data, assigning different levels of importance to different pieces. We each notice certain pieces of the human experience, and ignore others. On this, Prior cites author James K.A. Smith in his work *Imagining the Kingdom*, "Much of our action is not the fruit of conscious deliberation; instead much of what we do grows out of our passional orientation to the world—affected by all the ways we've been primed to perceive the world. In short, our action emerges from how we imagine the world."[11] So, Prior explains, "we perceive what we pay attention to."[12] And conversely, we fail to perceive what we don't pay attention to. In other words, we build our worldview out of what we think about. We think about what we notice. And we notice what we have been primed to notice. This is why it is crucial for us to train ourselves to notice data outside of how we have been primed.

Confirmation bias also affects how we interpret the Bible. How can Christians with the same Bible come to such radically different conclusions about what it really means, leading to the development of everything from high Catholicism to Amish theology? Putman quotes the late hermeneutics scholar Grant Osborne, "We rarely read the Bible to discover truth; more often, we wish to harmonize it with our belief system and see its meaning in light of our preconceived theological system."[13] So we pay attention to different pieces of the Biblical text, and we overlook, ignore, or reinterpret others. In other words, our confirmation biases often rule how

---

10 Rhyne Putman, When Doctrine Divides the People of God: An Evangelical Approach to Theological Diversity, (Wheaton: Crossway, 2020), 156.
11 James K. A. Smith, in Prior, *The Evangelical Imagination,* 13.
12 Prior, The Evangelical Imagination, 13.
13 Putman, When Doctrine Divides, 154.

we read Scripture. Someone raised Pentecostal will be primed to pay attention to certain verses, and someone raised Eastern Orthodox, different verses. Confirmation bias leads us to assign high import to the verses that confirm our theological systems, and to assign low import to the verses that don't.

Confirmation bias can also lead us to not even notice the data that fails to align with the theological interpretation we have inherited. For instance, I was taught for years that a biblical woman is a Proverbs 31 woman, and therefore that it would be sinful for me to work a job. I read Proverbs 31 many times during those years, yet it was not until I began questioning that theological framework that I even noticed that the Proverbs 31 woman *works a job*. She practices a trade (v. 13), engages in commerce (v. 18), buys land with her own income (v. 16), and sells goods in the marketplace (v. 24). My imaginative blinders prevented me from reading Scripture on its own terms. So if we desire to grow in knowledge of objective truth and not be limited by the chunk of stone we were born into, we must cultivate the art of paying attention.

Genuine listening helps us to be data-driven rather than system-driven. Being data-driven means that we are committed to analyzing the data of reality with as much objectivity as we can muster, being willing to adjust what we believe when confronted with new data. But being system-driven means that we will subconsciously ignore or downplay data that doesn't fit our preconceived system—systems such as our theological frameworks, our philosophical presuppositions, our political leanings, our theories of science, or our understanding of history. For instance, a committed atheist may be more likely to ignore or downplay evidence for theism. And a committed theist may be more likely to ignore or downplay evidence for atheism. The temptation for both is to uphold their system of thought over examining the data fairly. But a true love for truth means an openness to considering any observation about reality, even if it challenges our preexisting system.

The Value of Subjectivity

And so the value of subjectivity is revealed. Each of us has a different story. And our stories prime us to notice different things about the world we all share. Each of us brings something to the table. Each of us notices different verses of Scripture, or different news stories, or different social issues. This variety of emphases and perspectives can help us develop a richer, more expansive understanding of the fullness of reality, if we are willing to listen. C.S. Lewis lauds the value of learning from other perspectives in *An Experiment in Criticism*:

> The man who is contented to be only himself, and therefore less a self, is in prison. My own eyes are not enough for me, I will see through the eyes of others… In reading great literature I become a thousand men and yet remain myself. Like the night sky in the Greek poem, I see with a myriad eyes, but it is still I who see. Here, as in worship, in love, in moral action, and in knowing, I transcend myself; and am never more myself than when I do.[14]

Hence, open-mindedness is a crucial quality for seeking the truth about reality. Rightly practiced, it is the art and virtue of humility. It is the art of paying attention. At its best, it is the art of listening attentively to the insights of every person and every era, along with carefully identifying their associated blind spots and errors.

Is it worth learning from everyone? At minimum, every person possesses one crucial piece of data about reality that no one else in the history of the world has access to: namely, what it is like to be themselves. Of the billions of human beings that will ever exist—past, present or future—only one of them can speak with authority on what it is like to be yourself: you.

---

14 C.S. Lewis, *Experiment in Criticism* (Cambridge: Cambridge University Press, 2018), 140-141.

God's timeless, universal, changeless truth is contextualized in each of our unique lives. Transcendent truth does not change, but the way in which that truth is embodied is unique to each of us. So love asks that we listen well and glean what we can from those we encounter—if nothing else, that we may gain a deeper understanding of what it is like to live life in their shoes.

I would be remiss not to mention that empathy can, of course, be taken to an extreme. Our stories are, properly speaking, a mixture of facts and interpretations. And we don't always distinguish between these two. While the facts of our lives are unchanging, our interpretation of those facts may be misguided. For example, it is a fact that I have personally been harmed by Christians. But that fact could have multiple false interpretations, including that God hates me, that he approves of the harm I experienced, or that I would be right to reject Jesus. So we can gift someone with loving, empathetic presence without uncritically accepting any and every interpretation of the facts of their story. (Note well that even if someone's interpretation is incorrect, we should not presume to correct them unless we have the explicit invitation to share our own view.)

Even if someone is wildly misguided, we can still gain knowledge of what it is like to live in their shoes. Lewis again ponders the value of learning from other perspectives, calling it an act of love: "In love we escape from our self into one another." He continues, "We therefore delight to enter into other men's beliefs... even though we think them untrue. And into their passions, though we think them depraved... And also into their imaginations, though they lack all realism of content." This is "in order to see what they see, to occupy, for a while, their seat in the great theatre, to use their spectacles and be made free of whatever insights, joys, terrors, wonders or merriment those spectacles reveal."[15] Listening and learning, we imaginatively enter into each other's lived

---

15 Lewis, Experiment in Criticism, 139.

realities and continually seek to understand more data regarding reality and the human experience, even as we carefully distinguish between truth and error. To do so is an act of love.

Imagination allows us to empathetically listen to the truth our neighbor possesses: at minimum, what it is like to be themselves, and above and beyond that, their observations of culture and life that may ultimately need to inform our own views. We must listen to our physical and our intellectual neighbors with an ear towards any data we have not yet rightly considered. We must look for common ground, for things we may have missed. We must look for the things we have never before noticed.

Our individual stories and our collective memory inform our identities, our views of history, and our views of modernity. For instance, is the modern era good? It depends on your place in it, and the shape of your memory. If someone is descended from Mayflower pilgrims, she may view history and her place in it differently than a person descended from the enslaved, whose very surname and a portion of her genetics originate from a white, professedly Christian enslaver and rapist of her great-great-great-grandmother.

Our experiences also shape the data we notice. Someone raised conservative will be primed to notice data of a certain type, and someone raised liberal, data of a different type. A white pastor who has only had positive interactions with law enforcement may view certain public policy discussions differently than a black pastor who has had overwhelmingly negative interactions with law enforcement. A comfortably middle-class homeschooled suburban teenager may view government welfare differently than an impoverished urban teenager who has only survived childhood because of food stamps and free lunches through public school. A person who has experienced narcissistic abuse may be more likely to notice manipulative or abusive dynamics at church than a person who has never had personal experience with such dynamics.

What I'm Not Saying

When we point out the differences in perspective between, say, a rich person and a poor person, a white person and a black person, or an abused person and a non-abused person, I am not arguing that the person who is conventionally considered less "privileged" is automatically correct—or incorrect—about the topic at hand. This essay is not an affirmation of intersectionality, as if the person who has suffered the most in any given argument automatically "wins." However, this *is* an affirmation that various subjective life experiences provide unique data about objective reality that others may be ignorant of.

For example, as a woman, my experience of walking alone in the dark may be more negative than my husband's. My particularity and my subjectivity do hint at objective data about the dangers women experience, of which he lacks firsthand knowledge. But my "victim status" as female or my lack of "male privilege" does not mean I should automatically win every argument with my husband! My personhood transcends my victim status, putting us on equal footing as equal image bearers, equally capable of sin and virtue. Yet my subjective particularity does offer unique and immediate access to objective truths—immediate access that he lacks. As another example, we will fail to recognize objective realities of abuse within the church if we fail to prioritize listening to the people it most often affects, people whose experience at church differs from our own. There are aspects of objective reality that we will miss if we fail to listen to people with different experiences from our own.

Similarly, as a white, middle-class woman, I myself lack first-hand access to many aspects of objective reality. Like every person, I am contextualized in one context and not another. I have not experienced life as a racial minority or life under the poverty line. So there are aspects of objective reality that I will fail to understand if I do not take the time to listen to the subjective experiences of others unlike myself.

Again, this is not an affirmation of Marxism, critical race theory, or some other totalizing ideology only interested in deconstruction and reductionism. We are not defined *only* by our social categories, as if my entire identity could be reduced to my race, gender, or class. But it would be a mistake to think that these markers play *no* role in how we see the world—that is, the *data we notice* in the same objective world we share. Our socioethnic markers can be like blinders, guiding what data we notice and what data we either ignore or are ignorant of. So if we desire objective truth about reality, we must be willing to examine the subjective blocks of stone we originate from, the shape of the stone that underlies our perspective.

And affirming the value of individual perspectives does not entail the wholesale affirmation of postmodern relativism. We can affirm the value of individual perspectives without following postmodernism in claiming that *no* objective reality exists and that our individual relative "truths" are the *only* reality. In other words, individual perspectives offer us valuable data as we seek the truest understanding of objective reality, but they do not commit us to denying any form of objective reality.

Every one of us is beset by biases and prejudices. Sound reasoning is not merely a matter of syllogisms and logic. It also requires the careful consideration of the role of one's own subjective perspective in one's reasoning. Postmodernism highlights this crucial component of the reasoning process. While postmodern thought as a whole goes too far, inflating the role of subjectivity to the point that the objective is erased, we cannot thereby deny how great a role subjectivity does play in our reasoning processes. Our subjective stories and our relative viewpoints can and do highlight valuable data about the objective world.

Conclusion

The stunning real-world application is that our Amish neighbor, our Catholic neighbor, our Boomer neighbor, our pop-culture Generation Z neighbor, our urban neighbor, our rural neighbor, our Buddhist neighbor, our hyperconservative Christian fundamentalist neighbor, our deconstructing neighbor, our atheist neighbor, and our postmodern feminist neighbor may each have noticed valuable data about reality that we have ourselves missed. Amongst them all is a dizzying array of contradictory beliefs: truths dancing amidst falsehoods, like a diamond-studded coal mine. And each of us tend to have a predisposition towards which sorts of people we think possess more diamonds than coal. We may be correct. But even if someone possesses only one diamond in an entire vault of coal, that diamond is still precious, still valuable. All truth is precious. All truth is God's.

Used wrongly, our imaginations restrict our ability to access objective truth by limiting our ability to consider all the relevant data. But used rightly, our imaginations allow us to enter into a greater fullness of truth. We need subjectivity to achieve objectivity. We need postmodernism to achieve the goals of modernism. The diamonds of truth are worth mining for, no matter how dark the coal mine. And it is the work of Christ's presence to hospitably and empathetically make space for our neighbors' stories. It is truly a joy to embrace the *Imago Dei* in each of our neighbors and enemies, seeking natural revelation in unlikely places.

Let us, then, engage our world with humble curiosity and keen interest. We ought to always seek God's truth in every era, every field of thought, and in every human being. We must examine the data fairly, take our own biases and blinders into account, and let the data we discover continually flesh out our understanding of the fullness of reality. Let us value one another's stories and seek truth collaboratively, valuing the law of love above all. The journey of knowledge is lifelong. Like Michaelangelo's prisoners, may we be always becoming, until—praise be!—perfection comes, and the partial disappears.

Pink Faux Fur

Suzanne Carol

Individualities, chips broken from the social community of the historical past, are now allowed by modernity. The uniquenesses of individuals are becoming the building blocks of a robotic beast operated by remote control. However, the contemporary communal creature requires energy to run, and people are running out of fuel. Fortunately, the Word and Presence of God are most effective at the breaking point of humanism's promised structural strength. Released by grace from all collective control—secular and spuriously religious—the soul is freed to bathe in the life-giving blood of Christ and walk in The Way that He is.

In the courtyard behind a vape shop in a German biergarten, a young woman petted my pink fur sweater as if I were a bunny, laying her head on my shoulder in exhaustion. The firepit sparked behind us as restaurant staff left us to our conversation, knowing we would *eventually* be on our way. The night was chill, but not cold. The alcohol in her system softened her, but the Spirit of God drew her.

She was tired. Her guru had been filling her with humanistic pressures: "You are enough. You can do all things. You have the gift within. You are all you need."

She had been applying the costly sessions as best she could—even beyond her best, weakening rather than strengthening—and did I want to know a secret?

"I'm *not* enough," she whispered.

Shame trickled into my shoulder.

"I can't do it. I'm trying so hard, but I'm tired. *So* tired."

My pale pink faux fur dampened, either from the night air or her tears.

"You don't have to do it alone. You weren't *meant* to do it alone," I spoke gently so as not to spook this stranger who took to my side like cotton candy on a stick. The slightest harshness and I felt she would melt.

"I don't? Do you *mean* it? I don't have to do it all... *myself*?"

And there, the Spirit of God opened the scriptures of hope to an exhausted soul.

The chips of modernity are falling, humanism is failing, and some are doubling down. *But not all.* Some are disintegrating and finding hope beneath the rubble, a stream flowing behind the veneer of social media and social engineering, under the sands of newscasters and news spinners. The water flows. Draughts are drunk. God has not forgotten us.

Modernity's excitement of the individual through social spread, health and science breakthroughs, and media messages needfully breaks the historical collective that strong-arms us to follow simply because 'they say so'. More than tradition is necessary to hold us steady in an ever-changing world. We need the vital energy of life and life more abundantly, the very life that Christ, our ever-present shepherd, offers in His presence and by the gift of the extant Holy Spirit.

Shattering the peanut from the brittle, individuals need releasing from long-held bondages and patterns of thought and behavior soaked in the rum of unbelieving secrecy, sometimes veiled as faith and sometimes as atheism. Crimes are committed and victims are coerced to "keep it in the church" for the "sake of Christ's reputation," whisked behind the scenes and silenced for the Lamb.

Community resources of love, mercy, honesty, and justice are labeled "demonic influences of evil Babylon," while religious leaders offer little more than one could glean from a scroll through social media positivity memes: have hope, be sweet, be at peace (where there is no peace).

When the ligatures crack and modernity exposes motives and means, the structure totters, and even the Church (as it is represented) fails. This is good. The Church needs to be reminded that it is a gathering of individuals who follow The

Way; it is not The Way itself. The Church has the opportunity to be interested in the reputation of Christ Himself, rather than its business model. We will always need The Church, the elements of a greater whole, the members of His Body to gather, to teach, to love.

However, the Church, along with secular collectives, has (in growing cases) usurped the godhead and enthroned itself and its institutions as plastic monarchies, vulnerable to molding whims and cracking stress fractures. Collectivism itself was never designed to be The Answer. Christ Himself—an individual—was sent intentionally, deliberately, as The Answer, The Way.

The blood of the Lamb is not wheel grease to manipulate the political or parochial vehicles. Rather, it is our life. We bow before it, we bathe in it: from pulpit to pew, from pope to prostitute, from polished to punk. We are unique, we are precious each as each is. We needed modernity to remind us of this.

But we don't need modernity to capture our now splintered-off selves, becoming additions to *their* conglomerate metallic mass, architects of our own kind designing our collective fate. Instead, we need the Engineer of our Souls to recalibrate our compass with His Word, understanding scripture in context and according to the spirit in which it was given. We need our Savior to save us, each one, one by one, name by name, called and carried.

We need our tears felt on the downy, lambswool'd shoulder of compassion. We need to be reminded: we are each one unique, we were not created to accomplish life alone, our Creator has not abandoned us to a manufactured malfunctioning system of machine parts, secular or religious.

Modernity broke a moldy mass mold. *Thank God.*

Modernity released the individual. *Thank God.*

Modernity broke promises of structural integrity. *Thank God.*

God meets us in the rubble.

We sit cross-legged, brokenhearted, tired of trying,

trying, trying. The shadow of wooden beams falls on us as the light behind blinds us, exposing us. Our self-sacrifices are diluted by pride-filled intents. Our faint pink fur is only slightly dyed by the sweat of our own blood. And we lift our hands and cry, "Holy!," knowing the mirror has shattered. We see that we are seen.

The hide we need is His, ravaged scarlet flesh shredded by those of *our* ilk, *our* intent, *our* shame. His hide becomes our hiding place.

No longer protected by the collective, we raise our individuality to His hollowed-out wrist, insert our identifiable finger, and receive His welcome.

Modernity gave us the right to call ourselves by our names.

Christ gave us the right to become children of God.

BENT BINDING

Thomas Sims

This poem is initially a personal lament over the fragmentation that many of us face as a result of the current modes of living. Friendships from childhood rarely last until old age, and many friendships we form as adults are impoverished by ignorance of the friend's precious past. If, as Virgil wrote, "the best days are [in fact] the first to flee," then many of us never have the opportunity to live our best days together: hence the line "I either start on the hundredth or end on ninety-nine." The title plays on the multiple meanings of the word binding which can signify that which holds both a book and a friendship together. After all, it is equally as difficult to finish a book in our day and age as it is to see a friendship through to completion. While the poem does not directly address the substance of "modernity" as such, it expresses grief over the tangible effects of modernity upon human society, our consciousness and disposition towards time, and our personal relationships with each other. However, despite the unstable life conditions on which contemporary friendships are predicated, the poem ends on a hopeful note, indicating that like reading, friendships are still valuable in the face of the limits our lives impose on them.

Bent Binding

Starting a book on the hundredth page,
tragically late, a bewildered manticore in modernity
wondering at man in faithless age.
Fear makes cling to fragile certainty:

murdered myths on Reason's altar to ease troubled
   minds.

These days, authors often turn to platitude:
Tired clichés, an artistic capital crime:
A mass grave of malformed statuettes and
   misplaced gratitude.
They need shelter the sublime
or resign their work to propaganda and utility.

But, it's the hundredth page that's of much import.
I either start on the hundredth or end on ninety-
   nine.
Too late for the former, and the latter cut short,
to give all to both, if decision were mine,
to let both read me well, if only there were time.

Time: greedy glutton that gnashes all love spent,
good's limit, evil's relent, he denies vouchsafe to the
   page.
Battered books burn, or are broken, or bent.
For your sake, dear book, I address time in rage;
I wish to have grown up reading you and by you
   being read.

Inverting platitude, I've heard it said: "There's no
   friend like a good book."
As helplessly, from prologue to epilogue our
   forwards do contend,
With loving gaze at your pages frayed, despite all
   cruel time took,
at sage cliché, I boldly say: "No good book like a
   friend."

Reckoning with Death and Dying in a Disenchanted Age: The Christian Reality of the Fear of Death

Megan M. Starr

Introduction

Whether it occurs consciously or not, death holds sway as the central drama of human existence. Essentially, humankind, while varied in ethnicity, region, biological gender and age, shares one thing—all have a rendezvous with death. History highlights biblical truth: "for what happens to the children of man and what happens to the beasts is the same; as one dies, so does the other" (Eccl. 3:19). Sometimes one hears the Christian say they do not fear their mortal end, but most will honestly admit, to some degree, fear rears its ugly head when the topic of death arises or worse, when, in its nearness, it shakes the foundation of people's lives.

In the past, studies reveal those with a belief in God and a telos toward an eternity with him fear death less than their unbelieving counterpart. Yet a recent meta-analysis of religious studies and death anxiety provides contrary evidence. A team headed by Dr. Jonathan Jong, Research Associate of the Institute of Cognitive and Evolutionary Anthropology, gathered 100 published articles published between 1961 and 2014, most conducted in the United States. The team's finding "definitely complicates the old view," Jong admits, "that religious people are less afraid of death than nonreligious people."[1] Overall, results from the study show a

---

[1] University of Oxford, "News and Events," accessed April 25, 2023,

U-shaped trend, where both atheists and the very religious are those that do not fear death like those in the middle.[2] It is possible that the highly religious are now fewer in number while the atheists gained in number or that the atheists have increased greatly in number to meet the number of religious who fear death less than those in the middle. The majority of those in the middle are also of concern. Indeed, evidence shows it has, but *how* has our disenchanted age affected how we view death and grieve death and dying to produce the results given?

Perhaps a significant number of Christians have lost the firm foundation they once stood upon, believing in an afterlife and thus remaining content in all circumstances, including death. Further, it may be that the church wandered from the Christian reality of Christ's resurrection, a victory over death and sin. If so, what then is she believing? In fact, this trend may encompass the Christian who mourns with no hope.

Indeed, biblical grief and mourning remain an accepted and expected aspect when one encounters death. Christ represents grief while weeping over the grave of Lazarus and in the biblical practices surrounding death in early Christianity. However, the meta-analysis points to a change in the nature of the cultural disposition toward death for the believer, so to examine this in today's context, the current postmodern age, this essay looks at the culture, seeking not only the connection of the disenchantment of this age to its impact upon the Christian but also to that shift, as it happened sociologically, psychologically, and spiritually. The twenty-first century Christian believer must seek to reckon with death and dying in this disenchanted age and re-establish his ability to grieve with hope.

---

https://www.ox.ac.uk/news/2017-03-24-study-who-least-afraid-death.
2 Jonathan Jong, Robert Ross, Tristan Philip, Si-Hua Chang, Naomi Simons & Jamin Halberstadt (2018), "The religious correlates of death anxiety: a systematic review and meta-analysis," *Religion, Brain & Behavior*, 8:1, 4-20, DOI: 10.1080/2153599X.2016.1238844.

The Fog That Hangs Over Fatality

The previous study along with others and many cultural artifacts of the late twentieth and twenty-first century point to the reality of the rise of death anxiety in the United States. That is, the fear of death and the inability to cope with its repercussions, theologically. From statistics on popular funeral music to 'celebrations of life' held in lieu of funerals, to the literature, art, and film that pervades the current cultural landscape, one finds a culture that attempts to avoid the reality of death, but perhaps without even knowing, displays and engages in it everywhere, including the church.

The commercialization of the entire process of dying succeeds jointly with the expressive individualism of the day. According to James K.A. Smith, expressive individualism emerged from the Romantic expressivism of the latter half of the eighteenth century, and society is called to express or live out his or her own way of realizing one's humanity "rather than conform to models imposed by others (especially institutions)."[3] In the sanitized, consumer-driven funeral industry, personalized caskets exist, and the dead's favorite songs play, while families tuck special items into the caskets of the deceased. Primped and primed for a "viewing" in their Sunday best, the body lies cold and lifeless while the surrounding visitors fill the air with platitudes. Hid from view is the idea of death as it really is—the wages of sin, the final enemy, what Christ has crushed. Death is not a friend, nor are all the little deaths leading up to biological death; for these shadows are a part of the dark world of sin. The shadow of death, or fog over humankind's fatality, exists in knowing that death hangs over humans for the entirety of human existence. Clay Jones, professor, apologist and author of *Why Does God Allow Evil*, poignantly explains this shadow of death, brought about by the sin of Adam and Eve:

---

[3] James K.A. Smith, *How Not to be Secular: Reading Charles Taylor*, (Grand Rapids: William B. Eerdmans Publishing Company, 2014), 141.

> So the Lord cursed the ground, presumably enabling all kinds of pestilence, and then he kicked Adam and Eve out of the Garden, removing them from the rejuvenating power of the Tree of Life... and we've been attending funerals ever since.[4]

Sometimes it feels like a cascade of losses—these are experiences of the shadow of death. Each loss is a forerunner to the ultimate death of one's own body. Every glimpse of the shadow is a taste of mortality. These moments provide an opportunity to take an inventory and remember that this life is coming to an end; there is nothing friendly about that. The only friend in this scenario is the Savior. David remembers Him in Psalm 23, "even though I walk through the valley of the shadow of death," he cries, "I will fear no evil" (Psalm 23:4a); and again in Psalm 25 David's words remind the reader that it is not about us: it is about who God is, and it is "for your name's sake, O Lord" (Psalm 25:11). Our only hope is outside of ourselves; however, systematically, society continues the inward turn and focuses on the self.

From Where Does Expressive Individualism Come?

Carl Trueman, professor of biblical and religious studies at Grove City College, helps to draw out a consideration for anyone hoping to be a force for understanding people today and to remain good citizens who are faithful to Christ. His work suggests a way of "looking at the historical relationship between society at large and individual identity."[5] In the context of the funeral turned celebration of life, Trueman

---

4 Clay Jones, Why Does God Allow Evil: Compelling Answers for Life's Toughest Questions, (Eugene: Harvest House, 2017), 34
5 Carl Trueman, The Rise and Triumph of the Modern Self: Cultural Amnesia, Expressive Individualism, and the Road to Sexual Revolution (Wheaton: Crossway, 2020), 25.

casts a disparaging view, noting the meaninglessness that the celebration of life service promotes. He considers it "a nonsense… an insult to the bereaved relatives who, at best, are surely only kidding themselves that the death is made somehow easier by the fact the life was worth living in the first place."[6] To further his point, he considers this "a ridiculous contradiction in terms."[7] He contends, "if life has meaning, then death is an outrage; if death is not an outrage, then life has no meaning."[8] Furthermore, this contradiction flies in the face of the Christian understanding of death as the wages of sin, the price for which Christ paid. Death, however, looked upon to honor and exalt human life, presents death as meaningless, senseless, purposeless, therefore honors the individual and all his or her successes. Trueman also confirms that this sentimental postmodern view displays something different from the moderns. He finds it a symptomatic show of the vacuous nature of the most current age.

Furthermore, in additional works on the denial of death and death as the final enemy, Trueman brings both sex and death together showing that "earlier societies surrounded sex and death with sacred ceremonies, and for good reason: They cannot be trivialized, domesticated, or marginalized with impunity."[9] Relegating grief and lament to other occasions, the celebration of life ceremony creates an atmosphere that not only inhibits the mourning of family and friends but seeks to evade the reality of the significance of death altogether. One celebrates death like the rich man, the one who is considered a fool by God, who claimed, "I will say to my soul, "Soul, you have ample goods laid up for many years; relax, eat, drink, be

---

6 Carl Trueman, *Reformation 21* "Celebrating the Death of Meaning," accessed April 24, 2023, https://www.reformation21.org/counterpoints/celebrating-the-death-of-meaning.php.
7 Ibid.
8 Ibid.
9 *First Things*, "Deaths Delayed," March 31, 2020, https://www.firstthings.com/web-exclusives/2020/03/deaths-delayed.

merry."[10]

Additionally, in Manhattan's Metropolitan Museum of Art hangs El Greco's *Vision of St. John*, a painting from the seventeenth century which holds contemporary appeal. After the painting's "restoration" around 1880, nearly six feet were trimmed off the top half of the canvas. Representative of the opening of the fifth seal in Revelation 6:9, this work of art meant to reveal John looking up toward heaven while surrounded by a witness of faithful martyrs, is described by James K.A. Smith as "a fitting parable of modernity," where "the exultant arms of John the Revelator reach upward to— nothing: to the top of the frame, to the edge of the canvas. The martyrs seem to receive gifts from nowhere, and John seems to praise the nonexistent. All of them seem to look for something no longer there."[11] Smith teaches as a professor of philosophy at Calvin College and is known for condensing and clarifying the work of Charles Taylor. He readily explores the challenges of the aggressive secularism of today. Smith also suggests that the "modernist, secularist projects of 'improvement' have unwisely severed us from what makes for a flourishing society."[12] Counter to Smith's biblically relevant idea of a flourishing society, Chief Science officer, Aubrey de Grey of the Silicon Valley Research Foundation (SENS) believes "death must be approached not as the intractable end but as a tool to be taken out of the toolbox when it's convenient,"[13] and living each day with an awareness of death which shapes our life "seems antithetical to full human flourishing."[14] However, this disenchantment, or the lopping off of a sacred realm from humanity's understanding, is more than a worldview, it is a telos to nothingness. The disappearance of

---

10 Lk 12:19 (ESV).
11 James, K. A. Smith, *Comment*, "Cracks in the Secular," accessed April 29, https://comment.org/cracks-in-the-secular/.
12 Ibid.
13 J. Todd Billings, The End of the Christian Life: How Embracing Our Mortality Frees Us to Truly Live, (Grand Rapids: Brazos Press, 2020), 9.
14 Ibid.

the spiritual world, described by Taylor as "a world in which the only locus of thoughts, feelings, spiritual elan is what we call *minds*,"[15] is further delineated by Smith who says "the magical 'spiritual' world is dissolved and we are left with the machinations of matter"... a movement "from 'the world' into the mind."[16] By absorbing and living a disenchanted existence, as is evident of our current cultural climate through the work of Taylor, Smith, and Trueman, the Christian struggles to cultivate authentic Christian hope and face death biblically.

Inadequate Grief

The question then leads one to wonder to what degree the Bible-believing Christian is affected by this disenchantment of culture and to what degree can she remain as a faithful presence. Trueman's analysis of recent behavior is once again helpful in seeking answers to these questions. In a straightforward manner he claims that it is none other than the church's task to prepare our culture for death. Secular society (including Christians) in the West have become accustomed to "remarkably comfortable lives," Trueman quips, yet anxiety increased and displayed itself in fights over toilet paper in the grocery stores not long ago during the COVID crisis. And while "the task of the church (was) to mug people with reality before reality itself comes calling," she was "signally absent" during these months of hysteria.[17] [18]

One may also postulate that the eradication of an eternal or heavenly perspective implicit in one's current suffering and grief might underscore this absent reaction. Sociologist Jack B. Kamerman, expounds on the research of Robert Fulton on *Death and Identity*, and confirms this recent trend is a "shift in

---

15 Charles Taylor, *A Secular Age* (Cambridge: The Belknap Press of Harvard University Press, 2007), 29-30.
16 Smith, How Not to be Secular, 28.
17 Carl Trueman, "Deaths Delayed," *First Things*, March 31, 2020, https://www.firstthings.com/web-exclusives/2020/03/deaths-delayed.
18 Ibid.

the meaning of death from a process interpreted in a sacred framework to one interpreted in a secular framework."[19] [20] Kamerman also concludes, "without a sacred meaning to neutralize its evil, death has become almost 'dirty', not fit for polite society."[21] The streamlining of grief and mourning exists as a result. Indeed, grief renders itself unnecessary in this cyclical pattern. One removes the heavenly perspective and thought of a transcendent God, sovereign over his creation, then looks inward for consolation which cannot satisfy nor fill the void, therefore confirming his earlier premise of God's absenteeism and eternal nature. Death has been naturalized, and it has been handed over to the institutions, so the loss in rituals surrounding grief and the shortened time for mourning rationalize it. Consequently, if one's happiness resides solely in his or her present comfort, a biblical exegesis of 2 Corinthians becomes incomprehensible. Here, Paul addresses the Corinthians as he seeks unity from the church as he and Timothy sustained affliction from enemies in Asia. Paul exhorts:

> For we were so utterly burdened beyond our strength that we despaired of life itself. Indeed, we felt that we had received the sentence of death. But that was to make us rely not on ourselves but on God who raises the dead. He delivered us from such a deadly peril, and he will deliver us. On him we have set our hope that he will deliver us again.[22]

This hope is a recurring theme during suffering for Paul. He also reminds the Thessalonians about the coming of the Lord and works toward preparing them so that they are not

---

[19] Robert Fulton and Robert Bendiksen, editors, *Death and Identity*, (Philadelphia: Charles Press, 1976).
[20] Jack B. Kamerman, Death in the Midst of Life: Social and Cultural Influences on Death, Grief, and Mourning, (Englewood Cliffs: Prentice Hall, 1988), 7.
[21] Kamerman, Death in the Midst of Life, 7.
[22] 2 Co 1:8–10 (ESV).

uniformed about those who are asleep, that (they) may not grieve as others do who have no hope (1 Thess. 4:14).

Grieving over the loss of loved ones is a normal human experience, one in which even Jesus shared (John 11:35), "but the grief of Christians differs from that of unbelievers, for the latter have no hope of bodily resurrection to glory with Christ (1 Thessalonians. 4:16).[23] At least it should differ. In Truth, the remnants of a Christian-shaped social imaginary are fading fast and the new social imaginary replacing it exudes expressive individualism. In Trueman's further analysis, incorporating the work of Philip Rieff and Jean Jacques Rousseau, the complicit nature of the Christian is found in the expressive individualism of his place in the culture as he becomes "shaped by the expectations of the psychologized, therapeutic society in which we live, move, and have our being."[24] By tying together the cultural milieu of the sexual revolution and the expressive individualism which inhabits it, his work is pointedly true to the problem of death. Trueman examines a historical relationship between society and the individual. Consequently, the cultural implication of that relationship creates a necessary thread for also weaving together the contextual analysis of societal silence and denial of death which we see in the marginalizing of grief.

Marginalizing Death and Grief

Among the myriad of voices suggesting human flourishing can exist only when death is marginalized, J. Todd Billings, research professor of reformed theology, implores Christians who know better not to close "over the wound of death" but instead to be reminded to bear "witness to the Lord

---

[23] Thomas L. Constable, "1 Thessalonians, in *The Bible Knowledge Commentary: An Exposition of the Scriptures*, ed. J. F. Walvoord and R. B. Zuck, vol. 2 (Wheaton: Victor Books, 1985), 703.

[24] Carl Trueman, *The Gospel Coalition*, "Six Ways Christians Can Respond in Our Strange New World," July 11, 2022, https://www.thegospelcoalition.org/article/respond-strange-new-world/.

of creation who will set things right on the final day."[25] He urges the believer to acknowledge the 'cross-pressures' of what Charles Taylor calls our 'secular age', and "not to set (one's) Christian convictions on the shelf but to live into them, trusting that truth is possessed first and foremost by God."[26] In order to "reframe death" and "cultivate authentic resurrection hope," Billings claims that one must recognize that "Pushing away the reality of death is actually a form of slavery to the temporal, one that makes us cling to mortal life as though it will last forever or fulfill ultimate needs."[27] [28] For this, a deeper framework for understanding mortality over morbidity is required.

To do this, Billings incorporates the second century view of Irenaeus and his embrace of the creaturely stages of life where "dying itself can be part of a divine pedagogy for coming to know the mercy of the Lord;" it is, in this case, a welcome friend.[29] The fourth century view of Augustine, however, saw death as an enemy, an "irrational horror... a catastrophe, inherently violent and fundamentally unnatural."[30] For if the wages of sin is death (Rom. 6:23), it is the just punishment for sin. Somewhere within the complexity of this binary he seeks to find both to be true at the same time.

Upon receiving an incurable cancer diagnosis, as a theologian, young husband and father, Billings leaned more toward the Augustinian view in the beginning of his pilgrimage, but after interviewing multiple individuals who were believers at the end of a long life, he understood more the view of Irenaeus. Nevertheless, a forthcoming welcome near the end of life, may be due to the shadows of death throughout the lifespan. Feasibly, the fragility of elderly lives coupled with

---

25 Billings, The End of the Christian Life, 11.
26 Ibid., 15.
27 Ibid., 14.
28 Ibid., 12.
29 Ibid., 55-56.
30 Ibid., 59-60.

previous loss and inability to function wholeheartedly may lead to welcoming death. Recognized in songs and films regarding immortality, weariness wins. Even Roy Batty, the leader of the Nexus 6 replicants in the 1982 film *Blade Runner*, strives to meet his maker in a search of longevity, but recognizes the point at which his "accelerated decrepitude" meant it was "time to die."[31] At this point, one might consider death a "welcome friend," too.

With his own sense of living in the shadow of death, Billings reintroduces the Hebrew word *Sheol* in its Old Testament usage. It can be considered to mean "dark" (Lam 3:6), "dusty" (Job 17:16), "silent" (Psalm 31:17–18; 94:17), and "tempestuous" (Jonah 2:3–6)."[32] He goes as far as to say it is "a place of darkness, a prison for those who are silenced, cut off from life," but scripture is unclear if this "place" is a place of emotional abandonment (Psalm 86:1-13), or a place of the land of the biologically deceased, where one is cut off from the living and unable to return.[33] One might suggest that grief in death for the ones remaining may feel that they are the ones cut off, silenced, in a dark place and unable to return. Billings notes that one thing is sure, in either regard, no one can return from Sheol save for the will of God.

Additionally, reading the words of many of the psalmists, we can find multiple uses of this vast emptiness and thriving hope. This includes David's groaning in Psalm 22: "My God, My God, why have you forsaken me? Why are you so far from saving me, from the words of my groaning?" (Psalm 22:1). And later in verses 14-15:

> I am poured out like water,
> and all my bones are out of joint;
> my heart is like wax;
> it is melted within my breast;

---

31 Ridley Scott, 1982, *Bladerunner*, United States, Warner Bros.
32 D.A. Neal, "Sheol," ed. John D. Barry et al., *The Lexham Bible Dictionary* (Bellingham: Lexham Press, 2016).
33 Billings, The End of the Christian Life, 22.

my strength is dried up like a potsherd,
and my tongue sticks to my jaws;
you lay me in the dust of death.[34]

The Psalm is echoed again by Christ in his cry of dereliction in the gospels of both Matthew and Mark (Matt 27:46; Mark 15:34). Psalm 88 also describes aching and debilitating grief, mentioning Sheol:

For my soul is full of troubles,
and my life draws near to Sheol.
I am counted among those who go down to the pit;
I am a man who has no strength,
like one set loose among the dead,
like the slain that lie in the grave,
like those whom you remember no more,
for they are cut off from your hand.
You have put me in the depths of the pit,
in the regions dark and deep.
Your wrath lies heavy upon me,
and you overwhelm me with all your waves.[35]

For others outside of the grief, life continues, but for the one trapped in Sheol Billings says, "the attacker... has swallowed the living."[36] Sheol consumes.

Furthermore, Billings suggests that even when a Christian hopes to remain faithful in the face of death, there is a psychosomatic response beyond one's physical control. He claims, there is "something woven deeply into our created selves and our biological wiring."[37] Here, death-denial strategies and immortality projects arise. In grief, when death becomes this all-consuming pattern of existence, the only hope for the individual lies in repressing or negating it. For

---

34 *The Holy Bible*, Ps 22:14–15.
35 *The Holy Bible*, Ps 88:3–7.
36 Billings, The End of the Christian Life, 41.
37 Ibid., 73.

many people, including believers, these strategies and projects become the new normal. But the Christian knows that Jesus has delivered God's people from slavery to death and the fear of it. Therefore, the goal for the Christian life "is not eliminating the fear of death but removing death from its throne" so that they instead remember the promises of God and seek deliverance.[38] The burden lies on His shoulders when his people turn to him, "and only those who open their eyes in the place of darkness can see well enough to crave the resurrection light."[39]

Facing the Reality of the Pit

David Powlison, though his own walk with a cancer diagnosis which eventually ended his life, provides wisdom as an esteemed biblical counselor and previous director of the Christian Counseling Education Foundation (CCEF). Powlison taught that the Christian must, early on, face one's own mortality; they must face death with hope. Frequently teaching from Psalm 90, he suggests that through verses 1-11, we learn what death means. Then in verse 12, we are told "to number our days," that we may get a heart of wisdom so that God may establish the work of our hands.[40]

Likewise, the call for pastors is to "do the bulk of (their) theology when (they) are in the pulpit, so that when (they) are in the hospital room or in the living room and all around (them) is the wreckage of a calamity... they're not having to play a lot of catch up on theology or realizing that... I've never really trained these people to think well or to pray well in the midst of this sort of calamity."[41] Almost 350 years prior,

---

38 Billings, The End of the Christian Life, 76.
39 Ibid., 47.
40 David Powlison with Kevin Boling, "Facing Death with Hope," in *Knowing the Truth Radio*, produced by Sermonaudio, September 23, 2008, 4:47,
https://www.sermonaudio.com/solo/knowingthetruth/sermons/923081722100/
41 Todd Pruitt, "Mourn with those Who Mourn," in *Mortification of Spin*, produced by Reformation 21, April 26, 2023, 17:43.

Puritan Pastor Richard Baxter, did just that. He claims to have "preach'd as never sure to preach again, and as a dying man to dying men."[42] He encouraged others to plant, sow, and build, knowing they are "not (as) good as reaping, fruit-gathering, and dwelling; but in their season, they must be done."[43] Eternity permeated his life and his preaching. According to Billings, "in the Pit, we face a reality before which we are utterly impotent;" therefore, as Powlison, Baxter, and Billings concur, the people of God with open eyes to the reality of the Pit prior to living in it, sharpen their identity in Christ.[44] Reckoning with death reframes it in such a way as to remove it from the throne, to number one's days with authentic resurrection hope in Christ.

Conclusion

The first lines found in the materials used to research the topic of death appear profound. When the focus is on death, book after book and paper after paper trumpet edgy yet straightforward claims—"humans fear death;" "I am going to die;" "It cannot be that I ought to die;" but then came the one that announced what I didn't expect.[45] [46] [47] The first line that led to the premise that lies beneath the research question at the helm of this project: "Nothing I heard in the church helped."[48]

How can that be? I wondered. The core of the Christian

---

[42] J.M. Lloyd Thomas and N.H. Keeble, eds., *The Autobiography of Richard Baxter,* abridged (London: J.M. Dent & Sons, 1974), 26.
[43] Richard Baxter, *Dying Thoughts*, (Carlisle: Banner of Truth Trust, 2004), 3.
[44] Billings, The End of the Christian Life, 47.
[45] Clay Jones, Immortal: How the Fear of Death Drives us and What We Can Do About It, (Eugene: Harvest House, 2020), 19.
[46] David Gibson, Living Life Backward: How Ecclesiastes Teaches Us to Live in Light of the End, (Wheaton: Crossway, 2017), 11.
[47] Lloyd R. Baily Sr., *Biblical Perspectives on Death*, (Philadelphia: Fortress Press, 1979), 1.
[48] Lucy Bregman, *Beyond Silence and Denial: Death and Dying Reconsidered,* (Westminster John Knox Press: Louisville), 1999, 1.

faith rests in the resurrected hope in Jesus Christ. In a broken, debilitated world, much of the message of the Christian life consists of working out the implications of knowing the Creator of the universe in ways that also will make Him known to the world around us. Nowhere else can the believer meet the unbeliever on such firm, solid ground, then in death. Jaroslav Pelikan states it plainly: "A theology whose central message is the biography of a crucified Jew cannot avoid speaking about death, whether it be his or ours."[49] Writing in 1961, he engages the thoughts of five church fathers concerning death from the second and third centuries. We must wonder why the church of postmodernity, in a world vastly different from theirs, struggles simply to prepare *believers* to face death and dying, when the early church preached death and dying with "optimism and hope… to meet the pessimism of their pagan neighbors."[50] Thus, the question set forth at the outset of this essay was to determine not if, but how, the disenchanted age affects Christians' fear of death and dying as witnessed in their inability to lament with hope and speak boldly about it.

    The recognition of the presence of death anxiety among Christians—in fact, that it does exist and is on the rise in the current cultural climate, is the first step toward seeking the ways it has impacted Christianity in the West. Many studies have begun to point out the consumerism of the last century and its affect not only on what the society does and believes about death, but also how entwined Bible-believing Christians have become in the institutions that promote death as an intrusion to our comfortable lives and something to be dismissed, denied, and disguised. Confirming much of what this paper has covered, Fred Craddock believes that today, "Christians have ceded to others the scenario for dying… the church," he asserts "no longer has much to say or ways to say

---

49 Jaroslav Pelikan, The Shape of Death: Life, Death, and Immortality in the Early Fathers, (Nashville: Abingdon Press, 1961), 5.
50 Pelikan, The Shape of Death, 5.

convincingly those things it wishes to say."[51] Yet the evidence says she should.

To that end, the church must renew its place as the voice of truth, amidst a confused culture in a postmodern social imaginary that lacks not only reason but an understanding of the sacred. Placing a study in Ecclesiastes alongside a study of the current state of the American West shows there is nothing new under the sun, yet what remains beyond the materialism of this world exists and our longing for it, proclaims its presence to us. An analysis of the cultural artifacts of this generation speak to the hopes and desires that reside within. Marginalizing death and grief yield meaninglessness. Christians must speak to one another boldly on the topic of death and dying while walking with each other in lament and hope. As suggested by many of those referenced in this material, Psalms knits together lament and hope profoundly. The weight of the darkness of death and life in the pit may feel unbearable but it is not the time for hopeless despair, and it is not the time to stay silent in a hopeless world of chaos and confusion.

---

51 Fred Craddock, Dale Goldsmith, and Joy V. Goldsmith, *Speaking of Dying: Recovering the Church's Voice in the Face of Death* (Grand Rapids: Brazos Press, 2012), xvii.

Quiddity: A Dizain

Karise Gililland

Quiddity is a poem written in the Dizain form. The Dizain consists of ten lines, ten syllables a line, with a regular, mirrored rhyme scheme of ababbccdcd. Drawing an imaginary line between the last "b" and first "c" will help the pattern to emerge. In the first half, one "side of the mirror," if you will, the first and third lines rhyme, and the second, fourth, and fifth lines rhyme. Then, "reflected" in reverse, the second half of the poem uses this pattern, but backwards. The double letters, this time "c," come first, second, and fourth, with "d" coming in third and last.

This popular 15th-16th century French form was used in the 19th century by the Romantic poet, John Keats. Employed here, the form reflects the author's intention to reflect the Romantics' embracing of the sublime and supernatural in face of the determinism of the Enlightenment.

Quiddity is "the essence of a thing," that which makes it different from any other.[1] The poem begins by asking "Who is?" or "Who is he?;" it answers this question in the last line. The poet then takes us on an "etymological diversion" through the shifting landscape of "quis" and "quid" in Latin. The Latin word "quis" means "who." When "quis" shifts to the grammatical classification of gender neutered, it is a what, no longer a who. Thus, like ourselves, when cut off from identity, from our "who essence," the word devolves into a utilitarian "what." A "quid" is slang for the British pound, a currency. The idea of spending one's existence or bartering for meaning, reflected in modern self-identifying practices and constructs such as social media, where humans function as both consumers and products that are consumed. Thus the strange, third way of finding ourselves redefined as a what, a sort of

---

1 Oxfordreference.com

currency, neither necessarily male nor female, but as worthy as esteemed in trade only, then requires we be redeemed through an inequitable trade to be restored, (the *Full Quid*, not lacking) through the what, the word, that is a Who: The Word.

Quiddity

"the essence of a thing"
a Dizain

Quis est?[1] Et'mological diversion:
Who or what depends on connotation.
Gender neutered[2] becomes less a person;
Somehow losing ourselves in translation.
Tertium quid,[3] odd third situation-
Coined[4] word by word, bartered and rebranding.
Quiddity, one's pound of flesh withstanding,[5]
No equitable essence, *quid pro quo.*[6]
The Full Quid,[7] same essence left remanding,[8]
Word for words,[9] who supersedes *status quo.*[10]

---

1 Latin: "Who is?" or "Who is he?"
2 A play on words, referring to both the gender neutral classification of "quid" (what) as used for non-human things, and "quis" (who) used for people, being masculine or feminine; So quid (a thing) is obviously less than a person; when we deny our particular masculine or feminine humanity, we become as a thing; our Quiddity, or essence, that thing which is particularly human, our imago Dei, is lost.
3 Latin; Literally, "the third way;" refers usually to odd third parties or an ambiguous third way; indefinite but related somehow; the author uses this to refer to the neither male nor female status of the person as a what, a utilitarian, expendable, tradeable currency, as opposed to being a "who" that is particularly created imago Dei, in the image of God, as in Genesis 1:27b, "male and female He created them."
4 This double play on words refers to both the quid as slang reference to a British Pound, and to the modern re-invention of the self as some marketable, expendable identity or "brand" to trade upon.
5 "Pound of flesh": from Shakespeare's *Merchant of Venice*. The "pound of flesh" refers to Shylock's demanded payment for debt incurred. Double play on words as pound and quid are, as above referenced, interchangeable. This violation of essence, of trading being a "who for a what" requires some payment to redeem.
6 Latin; Literally, "something in exchange for something." In this case, the

required exchange to restore or redeem a mistaken identity, literally the wrong essence by definition; once misappropriated, some other, fuller essence must be given in exchange for that pound of flesh; references the Incarnation (John 1:14); withstanding: references the death, burial, and resurrection of Jesus (Luke 24:7).
7 The Full Quid: slang referring to a full payment; conversely, "not the full quid" is to be lacking mentally. In this case, a full, complete, true payment must be made.
8 Remanding: legal; to send back into custody, await further proceedings.
9 Word for words: Trading him that is fully God and fully man, a "who," the Word, (Jesus, John 1:1), for the coined and bartered "what" words (identities) that men and women have put upon themselves in separating themselves from God
10 Latin, meaning "existing state of affairs;" In this case, the Word, Jesus, supersedes our fallen and mortal state, that status quo; answers the first line, "Who is He?"

Pious Transaction or Blessed Exploit? Theologies of Nature from Paganism to Modernity

Jason Smith

Almost since the modern environmentalist movement re-began in the 1960s, the legacy of Christian tradition and the activism of various contemporary Christian groups have together been blamed for causing, exacerbating, denying, obfuscating, and actively colluding with the global ecological crisis.

A seminal paper published in *Science* in 1967 by medievalist Lynn White laid out the paradigm-establishing critique:

> What did Christianity tell people about their relations with the environment?... [that] God planned all of this explicitly for man's benefit and rule: no item in the physical creation had any purpose save to serve man's purposes. And, although man's body is made of clay, he is not simply part of nature: he is made in God's image. Especially in its Western form, Christianity is the most anthropocentric religion the world has seen... Man shares, in great measure, God's transcendence of nature. Christianity... not only established a dualism of man and nature but also insisted that it is God's will that man exploit nature for his proper ends.
>
> ...At the level of the common people this worked out in an interesting way... By destroying pagan animism, Christianity made it possible to exploit nature in a mood of indifference to the feelings of natural objects.

> ...Both our present science and our present technology are so tinctured with orthodox Christian arrogance toward nature that no solution for our ecologic crisis can be expected from them alone... Hence we shall continue to have a worsening ecologic crisis until we reject the Christian axiom that nature has no reason for existence save to serve man.[1]

To overstate the audacity of these claims presents a challenge. In a few sentences, White appears not only to radically mischaracterize Christianity, but dualism (which predates Christianity and has often been syncretized with it) and animism as well.[2][3] That making use of a particular grove, grotto, fountain, or tidepool for trade or agrarian purposes in pagan antiquity may have first required propitiating its patron deity or *genus loci*, even to consecrate it as a sort of classical nature preserve, is not the same as having empathy for or recognizing value in nature itself. A healthy fear of guardians, coupled with a ritualized means of placating those guardians, is not *per se* greatly removed from the hunting licenses and development permits of modern society. It is not self-evident that the transactional relationship between these pagan "common people" and their local deities is superior to, or even much different from, the more explicitly utilitarian relationship between man and nature that White mistakenly identifies as Christian.

Yet the paper rapidly gained widespread hearing. As its influence spread, White's accusations could have and should have been challenged and corrected—on theological grounds, historical grounds, and ultimately through the overwhelming

---

[1] Lynn White, *et al.* "The Historical Roots of our Ecological Crisis," *Journal of the American Scientific Affiliation*, June 1969,
http://www.asa3.org/ASA/PSCF/1969/JASA6-69White.html.
[2] Ugo Bianchi & Matt Stefon, "dualism", *Encyclopedia Britannica Online*, Dec. 13, 2022. https://www.britannica.com/topic/dualism-religion
[3] One is tempted to speculate quite uncharitably about White's decision to publish these assertions in a science rather than humanities journal!

counterexample of believers' behavior. His critique ought not to have been allowed to stand.

But something different seems to have happened instead. In a 2015 article for *The Christian Century*, environmental historian Mark Stoll asserts that although "White's essay prompted soul-searching in mainline Protestant churches," resulting in a "greening" of their theology, in the 1970s "Evangelical anti-environmentalism appeared" in response.[4]

Such reactionism could be read as consistent with the 20th-century Anglo Protestant Mainline/Evangelical conflict. Evangelical missiologist Ralph Winter says that the focus of American Protestant outreach in the 20th and late 19th centuries became characterized by "a distinct polarization... [especially evident] in the Fundamentalist/Modernist controversies of the 1920s." Winter describes this conflicted Protestant missional ethos as "an artificial tension between saving souls and saving souls *plus* saving people, society, and nature"—a division which "became virulent in the 20th century."[5]

But Stoll suggests that Evangelicals are reacting to cultural movements outside of Protestantism also. He says that White's introduction and/or popularization of

> The idea that Christianity has been antithetical to environmentalism also inspired many to seek greener spirituality in Eastern and indigenous religions. Neo-paganism and earth-centered spiritual thought grew popular. Evangelicals recoiled from environmentalism and charged that environmentalists worshipped creation rather

---

[4] Mark Stoll, "The Historical Roots of Evangelical Anti-Environmentalism," *The Christian Century*, June 2015, https://www.christiancentury.org/blogs/archive/2015-06/historical-roots-evangelical-anti-environmentalism.

[5] Ralph Winter, "Three Mission Eras and the Loss and Recovery of Kingdom Mission, 1800-2000," in *Perspectives on the World Christian Movement: A Reader*, eds. Ralph D. Winter and Stephen C. Hawthorne (Pasadena: William Carey Library, 2009), 265-266.

than the Creator. In the late 1970s they seized on the notion of the 'culture wars' and lumped environmentalism together with abortion, feminism, gay... rights, and secular humanism as contrary to Christianity [and have been] hostile to environmentalism ever since.[6]

Theologian Scott Rodin's personal experience agrees with Stoll. In 2015, Rodin published a renunciation of his life-long denial of climate change science to his blog, *The Steward's Journey*, in which he discussed five modes of thinking that decades of being a "Conservative, Evangelical, Republican" had conditioned him to. Among them: "As a conservative Christian, if you even hinted at 'caring' for creation, you were already heading down the slippery slope of pantheism."[7]

Meanwhile Catholics, along with mainline Protestants, seem to have agreed with White's historical interpretation as well as his terms of theological indictment. In 1979, Pope John Paul II declared Francis of Assisi the Patron Saint of Ecology—something White's paper had explicitly called for ten years prior. More recently, reporting for *The Washington Post* on President Trump's decision to withdraw from the Paris Climate Agreement, Sarah Pulliam Balley quotes Pope Francis' 2015 Encyclical on the environment as calling for

> an "ecological conversion," saying Christians have misinterpreted Scripture and "must forcefully reject the notion that our being created in God's image and given dominion over the earth justifies absolute domination over other creatures."[8]

---

[6] Stoll, "The Historical Roots of Evangelical Anti-Environmentalism."

[7] Scott Rodin, "As a Conservative, Evangelical Republican, Why Climate Change Can't be True (Even Though It Is)," *The Steward's Journey*, 2015, http://thestewardsjourney.com/as-a-conservative-evangelical-republican-why-climate-change-cant-be-true-even-though-it-is/.

[8] Sarah Pulliam Bailey, "Why So Many White Evangelicals in Trump's Base Are Deeply Skeptical of Climate Change," *The Washington Post,* June 2017, https://www.washingtonpost.com/news/acts-of-faith/wp/2017/06/02/why-so-

Despite the nearly fifty years intervening, such wording could hardly have been better chosen to directly engage White's critique—yet it does so apparently from a position of tacit agreement.

An exhaustive treatment of Christianity's contributions and responses to environmentalism is beyond the scope of this essay. However, by refocusing attention on the "classical consensus" tradition of Christian theology, this essay will address not only White's misrepresentations of Christian teaching (and, by implication, Christians who may have too-hastily accepted his views), but also the misguided Evangelical or Fundamentalist reaction, which has served (through confirmation bias) to "prove" White's critique *post facto*.

Confessional vs. Lived Belief

Objections to White's paper were raised from within the Christian tradition almost immediately. For example, at an American Scientific Affiliation Annual Convention panel specifically organized to respond to the paper just a few months after its publication, respondents noted that White's understanding of Christian 'dominion' teaching was dangerously incomplete: "The answer lies not in rejection of one Biblical teaching but rather in acceptance of entire Biblical doctrine." White's "description of the teachings of Christianity" was described as "partially confused." One even asserted, "There is no way that an evangelical Christian can biblically justify an indifference to the exploitation of nature."[9]

However, as we have already noted, these and other objections seem to have made little lasting impression on the unfolding debate. One panelist's admission helps explain why:

> The article's erroneous statements seem to stem

---

many-white-evangelicals-in-trumps-base-are-deeply-skeptical-of-climate-change/.
9 White, *et al,* "The Historical Roots of our Ecological Crisis."

from White's main heretical concept that there is a "Christian axiom that nature has no reason for existence save to serve man." Such a statement *could* result from a study of the behavior of 'Christianized' peoples...[10]

As T.S. Eliot observes in his 1940s-era *Notes Towards the Definition of Culture*, "what we believe is not merely what we formulate and subscribe to, but... behaviour is also belief." He continues, "even the most conscious and developed of us live also at the level on which belief and behaviour cannot be distinguished."[11] While the panelist quoted above wishes that White had addressed "disparity between behavior and... Biblical truth," Eliot would have understood such disparity as reconciled within a group's culture, evidencing its true creed.[12] [13] He might have called it *lived belief*.

Unsound in several other respects, White's paper was right to criticize Christendom for its *lived belief* toward nature. The erosion of pagan animism, combined with the progression from natural theology's "the decoding of the physical symbols of God's communication with man" into modern science's "effort to understand God's mind by discovering how his creation operates" did indeed set the table for Baconian appetites for the subjugation of nature, the modern scientific method, and (eventually) the Industrial Revolution—in short, for the capacity and execution of extraordinary near-term gains in improving human material conditions at the cost of long-term peril for the natural world (and humanity itself), largely through externalities and

---

10 Ibid. Emphasis added.
11 T.S. Eliot, *Notes Towards the Definition of Culture*, (Digital Library of India, 2015), https://archive.org/stream/in.ernet.dli.2015.159230/2015.159230.Notes-Towards-The-Definition-Of-Culture_djvu.txt.
12 White, *et al*, "The Historical Roots of our Ecological Crisis."
13 Eliot admits this insight is "disconcerting," "disturbing," and "embarrassing," difficult to "contemplate long without horror," and advises meditation on "the possibility of grace and the exemplars of sanctity in order to avoid falling into despair."

unintended consequences.[14] [15]

However, this centuries-slow and deadly creep of philosophical outlook aiding and abetting technical prowess was not, as White's paper erroneously claims, 'orthodox'. Systematic theologian Thomas Oden, venturing to speak on behalf of the "classic consensus" of foundational Christian writers, draws on Peter, Barnabas, Tertullian, Luke, Origen, Athanasius, Basil, and Calvin for the following summary of Christian teaching:

> Humanity is given dominion and stewardship over the earth... according to Hebraic religion... "You shall have dominion" (Gen. 1:26, 28) implies that you take care of it. God entrusts the world to your care and benefit. In the guardianship of this fragile world you are called to respond fittingly to the One who gives and transcends all creaturely values. Humanity is called to order the world rightly under the permission and command of God... to shape the world in a fitting response to God's unpurchasable gift of life. All this is implied in the notion of stewardly dominion... Nature is to be greatly respected, nurtured, and cared for, but not worshiped.[16]

But, despite being laid out plainly from long before the inception of the Church, this message was slow to penetrate the pagan culture of Europe. C.S. Lewis explained in a series of Oxford lectures on medieval thought that "Though Christians were logically bound to admit the goodness of matter [*i.e.* nature] that doctrine was not heartily relished... for centuries, the language of some spiritual writers was hardly to be

---

[14] White, *et al*, "The Historical Roots of our Ecological Crisis."
[15] cf. Eugene Schwarz, Overskill: The Decline of Technology in Modern Civilization.
[16] Thomas Oden, *Classic Christianity: A Systematic Theology* (New York: HarperOne, 1992), 138.

reconciled with it."[17]

Writing more recently, David Bentley Hart explains,

> Christian thought taught that the world was entirely God's creature... a gratuitous work of transcendent love, it was to be received with gratitude, delighted in as an act of divine pleasure, mourned as a victim of human sin, admired as a radiant manifestation of divine glory, recognized as a fellow creature; it might justly be cherished, cultivated, investigated, enjoyed, but not [in contrast to pagan antiquity] feared, not rejected as evil or deficient, and certainly not worshipped.[18]

Yet Hart agrees with Lewis that though these "revisions of human thought... occurred at every level of society," they did so "gradually, irregularly, [and] imperceptibly."[19]

In short, it was a failure of Christian orthodoxy, not a triumph, that allowed some in the Christianized West to believe that the natural world existed expressly for humans to exploit as they saw fit. White himself seems to have based his assertion of "orthodoxy" for the views criticized by his paper on the mistaken claim that St. Francis of Assisi's ecological sympathies, his "belief in the virtue of humility not merely for the individual but for man as a species," were somehow "clearly heretical"—thus, any view which aggrandizes humankind, however extreme, must presumably be 'orthodox'.[20] Yet White offers scant evidence to support either assertion. Had a false equivalence not, after all, risen in the popular mind between divinely-sanctioned human *dominion* versus *domination* of nature, we would suspect the so-called 'Christian' narrative which White condemns to be his own invention.

On one hand, we might justly excuse the Church for its

---

17 C.S. Lewis, *The Discarded Image* (Cambridge University Press, 2015), 51.
18 David Bentley Hart, *Atheist Delusions* (Sheridan: Ann Arbor, 2009), 212-213
19 Ibid., 212
20 White, *et al*, "The Historical Roots of our Ecological Crisis."

tardy opposition to that false equivalence: Until quite recently, domination was entirely beyond human technical capacity. Confusion of terms, though figuratively harmful, was literally inconsequential. Actual domination of nature was for centuries no more than the toothless pipe-dream of a few delusional eccentrics. During all of recorded history prior to the nineteenth century, it had been humanity that needed to fence itself off, that needed protection, from nature. When the reversal occurred, it became so far-reaching so quickly that we are still struggling to understand it. It has been proposed that we may have accidentally created a new geologic era—the Anthropocene—or even a new geologic epoch—the Anthropozoic. Writing for *The Scientific American* in 2014, Clive Hamilton explains,

> The arrival of the new epoch represents not merely the further spread of human influence across the globe but a fundamental shift in the relationship between humans and the Earth system—one in which human activity now accelerates, decelerates and distorts the great cycles that make the planet a dynamic entity.[21]

This reversal of planetary-scale power dynamics happened with (anthropologically speaking) blinding speed, accompanied by a bewildering array of unforeseen social and cultural changes ushered in by the Industrial Revolution.

And yet, conservation movements arose concurrently with—and even anticipate—technological exploitation of the natural world, in the very same Christianized West that White faults for environmental immorality based on supposedly 'Christian' teaching.[22] [23] In the nineteenth and early twentieth

---

21 Clive Hamilton, "The New Environmentalism Will Lead Us to Disaster," *The Scientific American,* June 2014, https://www.scientificamerican.com/article/the-new-environmentalism-will-lead-us-to-disaster/.
22 *cf.* John Evelyn's 1662 Royal Society presentation 'Sylva'.
23 cf. Evan Berry's 2015 book Devoted to Nature: The Religious Roots of American Environmentalism.

centuries the conservation movement's setbacks came, not from Christianity, but from *laissez-faire* economic theory and concern for private-property rights. Casting his eye back over the preceding century, Eliot keenly observes in a 1939 companion lecture to the aforementioned *Notes*,

> We are being made aware that the organization of society *on the principle of private profit...* is leading both to the deformation of humanity by unregulated industrialism, and to the exhaustion of natural resources, and that a good deal of our material progress is a progress for which succeeding generations may have to pay dearly... the exploitation of the earth, on a vast scale for two generations, for commercial profit: immediate benefits leading to dearth and desert.[24]

On the other hand, to those suffering from exploitation or its effects, parsing the exact sources of our ecological crisis would surely sound a purely semantic or ivory-tower exercise: Bickering, blame-shifting, producing distinctions without practical differences. Indisputably, the weight of Christendom's and post-Christendom's *lived belief* has fallen crushingly upon the world. From this lived belief many branches of the Church seek repentance; within that perspective, we can certainly understand and sympathize with the official responses and activities of mainline Protestants and Catholics in recent decades.

But what are we to make of the Evangelical reaction?

Tangled Identities

At first glance, it almost looks as if Evangelicals embraced White's caricature of Christianity as gospel truth. If one wants to "prove" White's paper correct, one need look no further than Evangelical anti-environmentalism before issuing a

---

[24] T.S. Eliot, "The Idea of a Christian Society," in *Christianity and Culture* (New York: Harcourt, Brace and World, 1949), 58. Emphasis added.

hasty verdict. The impression thus begets a straw-man against which such caricatures of Christianity can be easily perpetuated, while also smearing into incomprehensibility what is actually a loose conglomerate of positions—some theological, others only nominally Christian; some in fierce disagreement on certain points and allied in others.

In actuality, there is no unified or codified Evangelical anti-environmentalism movement. There are only, on the one hand, Evangelicals averse to certain philosophical strains of environmentalism on theological grounds; and on the other, conservatives averse to certain kinds of environmental policy on political grounds, some of whom also self-identify as Evangelical (about 40 percent, according to the Pew Research Center).[25] As this paper's particular concern is with Christian environmentalism *per se*, we will spend a minimum amount of time addressing conservative environmental politics so as to be able to consider Evangelical theological teaching with less confusion. Such disentangling will not solve for Evangelical *lived belief* which, like that of every Christian culture as a whole, remains problematic to whatever extent it is insufficiently Christian. But it may help clarify the situation for those without and within Evangelical tradition.

Primary among conservative objections to environmentalism is suspicion of 'big government' as a provider of solutions (regulatory, service-based, and otherwise). A corollary contention concerns whether climate change and habitat destruction leading to less hospitable ecologies, or top-down economic regulation that may lack local insight and focus, poses the greater threat to the poor and least-advantaged. On these points, there's little real quarrel with conservation or pro-environment goals; the debates are

---

25 Pew Research Forum, "Religious Landscape Study: Conservatives," (2014), http://www.pewforum.org/religious-landscape-study/political-ideology/conservative/.

strictly about methods.[26] [27] Whether there is an intrinsically Christian root to these political stances is a question for a different paper. Here we must simply acknowledge that this is a factor for political conservatives and recognize its distinction from both environmentalism as such and Christianity as such. Confusion on this matter stems from the overlap between Evangelicalism and conservatism, an arena where Christian verbiage and Bible verses are commonly used to justify public policy positions or solicit political support.

This is problematic from the standpoint of *lived belief*:

> according to Katharine Hayhoe, an atmospheric scientist at Texas Tech University who does climate change education among evangelicals... "Somehow, evangelicalism got politicized to the point where, [for] many people who call themselves evangelicals, their theological statement is written by their political party first."[28]

In fact, "after taking politics and demographics into account," a 2015 Pew Research Center analysis found that "religious affiliations and practices have little connection to most attitudes toward the environment."[29] This suggests, once again, that even among Evangelicals the problem isn't one of Christian *doctrine*, but rather of the failure of that doctrine to adequately penetrate—to be fully understood, accepted, and lived out.

---

26 Sean McElwee, "Can We Make Environmentalism a Centrist Issue?" *The American Prospect*, March 2014, http://prospect.org/article/can-we-make-environmentalism-centrist-issue.
27 *cf.* Stoll, Rodin, Bailey.
28 Bailey, "Why So Many White Evangelicals..." etc.
29 Sarah Pulliam Bailey, "Religion Doesn't Necessarily Influence Americans' Attitudes About Science," *The Washington Post*, October 2015, https://www.washingtonpost.com/news/acts-of-faith/wp/2015/10/22/religion-doesnt-necessarily-influence-americans-attitudes-about-science-but-there-are-two-big-exceptions/.

But there are exceptions. Heterodox environmental theologies, based on alternative interpretations of key scriptures, persist in popular and clerical creeds. Some even resemble those that White's paper decried.

Protology: Fearing Loss of Dominion

One major area of concern for so-called 'anti-environmentalist' Evangelicals is a perceived incompatibility between essential understandings of humans and nature. These Evangelicals see the modern environmentalist movement as variously mischaracterizing:

- Humans as problem-causers, rather than problem-solvers;[30]
- The moral claims of the natural world as equal to or greater than the moral claims of fellow humans;[31]
- The spiritual claims of the natural world as worthy of worship and service (as in pantheism, new age

---

[30] "Where environmentalists start off as fundamentally mistaken is their vision of human beings. They see human beings as, primarily, consumers and polluters. Whereas the Bible teaches that humans, who are made in God's image, are producers and stewards. Obviously, it's not automatic. There needs to be education and moral commitment, and those things are furthered in my understanding through people being reconciled to God through the atoning work of Christ on the Cross and their faith in Him. As the late Julian Simon used to put it: 'Every mouth that is born into this world is accompanied by two hands and, far more importantly, a mind.' Those two hands and a mind are capable of producing far more than that mouth can consume." Calvin Beisner, spokesman of evangelical anti-environmental advocacy group The Cornwall Alliance. Quoted by Leo Hickman in "The U.S. Evangelicals Who Believe Environmentalism is a 'Native Evil'," *The Guardian,* May 2011, https://www.theguardian.com/environment/blog/2011/may/05/evangelical-christian-environmentalism-green-dragon.

[31] "Whereas, Some in our culture have… elevated animal and plant life to the place of equal—or greater—value with human life… we oppose solutions… which bar access to natural resources and unnecessarily restrict economic development, resulting in less economic opportunity for our poorest citizens." 2004 Statement of the Southern Baptist Convention on "Environmentalism and Evangelicals," quoted by Mark Stoll in "The Historical Roots of Evangelical Anti-Environmentalism" (*op. cit.*)

paganism, and other forms of earth-worship or reverence for an impersonal life-force);[32]

- Human intervention in the natural world as necessary because God doesn't exist and/or won't intervene on his creation's behalf.[33] [34]

Each of these mischaracterizations would seem to challenge the Christian understanding of humankind's divinely-appointed *dominion* over nature, as described in the Genesis creation accounts and elsewhere. Where many believers—such as mainline Protestants, Catholics, and in recent decades, some Evangelicals—have taken an "act now, preach right doctrine along the way" approach to environmentalism, many Evangelicals insist on addressing these concerns first so as to lay a proper theological foundation for understanding the challenges faced and how best to answer them.[35] [36]

While this approach is very much in keeping with a conservative outlook generally, it can also be read as part of a specifically-Evangelical attempt to shield Evangelical understanding of the Bible and biblical authority from interpretative challenges made by untrustworthy "secular"

---

32 *cf.* Stoll, Rodin.
33 "[Many of] the evangelicals Veldman has spoken to oppose... [man-made or man-solved] climate change because they see it as a threat to God's omnipotence." Bailey, "Why So Many White Evangelicals..." (*op. cit.*)
34 "The idea that God will fix climate change —or that trying to curb its impact is an affront to the divine—is a common refrain among Republican politicians." Jack Jenkins, "Lawmaker Thinks God Will 'Take Care' of Climate Change if it Becomes a 'Real Problem'," *ThinkProgress*, June 2017, https://thinkprogress.org/lawmaker-climate-change-god-bf84a114b557.
35 *cf.* John Collins Rudolf, "An Evangelical Backlash Against Environmentalism," *New York Times*, February 2010
https://green.blogs.nytimes.com/2010/12/30/an-evangelical-backlash-against-environmentalism/
36 Tik Root, "An Evangelical Movement Takes On Climate Change," *Newsweek*, March 2016,
http://www.newsweek.com/2016/03/18/creation-care-evangelical-christianity-climate-change-434865.html.

authorities, which potentially includes both political leaders and research scientists. Historian Molly Worthen, writing on "The Evangelical Roots of Our Post-Truth Society" for *The New York Times* in April, says,

> Ever since the scientific revolution, two compulsions have guided conservative Protestant intellectual life: the impulse to defend the Bible as a reliable scientific authority and the impulse to place the Bible beyond the claims of science entirely. The first impulse blossomed into the doctrine of biblical inerrancy… The second impulse, the one that rejects scientists' standing to challenge the Bible, evolved by the early 20th century into a school of thought called presuppositionalism… Cornelius Van Til, a theologian who promoted this idea, rejected the premise that all humans have access to objective reality. "We… do not grant that you see any fact in any dimension of life truly," he wrote in a pamphlet aimed at non-Christians… By contrast, the worldview that has propelled mainstream Western intellectual life and made modern civilization possible is… an empirical outlook that continually—if imperfectly—revises its conclusions based on evidence available to everyone, regardless of their beliefs about the supernatural.[37]

The desire to uphold orthodox protology, to promote biblical understanding of humanity's role as stewards of God's good creation according to the pattern God set, is a commendable desire. But perhaps White (and many others since) have been right to criticize the Evangelical focus. Perhaps Evangelical priorities reveal heterodox theological

---

37 Molly Worthen, "The Evangelical Roots of our Post-Truth Society," *The New York Times,* April 2017
https://www.nytimes.com/2017/04/13/opinion/sunday/the-evangelical-roots-of-our-post-truth-society.html

concerns in need of course-correction. At minimum, it seems to this writer that the zeal and energy employed making claims about humanity's divine status as creation stewards might be better spent demonstrating it. If we truly want good for our world, we don't need to first agree about why.

Eschatology: Anticipating the End of Creation

Of greater concern are misunderstandings of Christian eschatological teaching. Theologian N.T. Wright has addressed these in an elegant article for *Plough* titled "Jesus is Coming—Plant a Tree!" The problem, he says, is that

> Western Christianity has allowed itself to embrace that dualism whereby the ultimate destiny of God's people is heaven, seen as a place detached from earth, so that the aim of Christianity... is seen in terms of leaving earth behind and going home to a place called heaven. So powerful is this theme in a great deal of popular preaching, liturgy, and hymnography that it comes as a shock to many people to be told that this is simply not how the earliest Christians saw things. For the early Christians, the resurrection of Jesus launched God's new creation upon the world, beginning to fulfill the prayer Jesus taught his followers, that God's kingdom would come "on earth as in heaven"... The question of how you think about the ultimate future has an obvious direct impact on how you think about the task of the church in the present time.[38]

Indeed. And if one believes or is taught that the natural world is destined for destruction, a messy slate waiting to be

---

38 N.T. Wright, "Jesus is Coming—Plant a Tree!," *Plough*, 2015, http://www.plough.com/en/topics/justice/environment/jesus-is-coming-plant-a-tree.

wiped clean, one has little motivation to improve anything that doesn't serve one's own personal needs. Such thinking is a recipe both for apathy towards the environment, and for pity, contempt, and resentment towards those who attempt to raise awareness and resources for efforts that, on this account of the situation, can amount to no more than expensive itch-cream on a wounded limb due for amputation.

The corrective for such theological imbalance, according to Wright, is to follow the original orthodox teaching of the Church, which

> clung to the twin doctrines of creation and judgment: God made the world and made it good, and one day he will come and sort it all out. Take away the goodness of creation, and you have a judgment where the world is thrown away as so much garbage, leaving us sitting on a disembodied cloud playing disembodied harps. Take away judgment, and you have this world rumbling on with no hope except the pantheist one of endless cycles of being and history. Put creation and judgment together, and you get new heavens and new earth.[39]

Expecting the return of Christ, the renewal of creation, and the earthly descent of the New Jerusalem as described in Revelation 21, encourages Christians to interpret the dominion mandate of Genesis 1 and 2 in light of teaching on God-honoring stewardship that runs throughout Scripture. That we will be judged for our treatment of the material entrusted to us—our time, talents, and treasure, as well as our words, thoughts, and deeds—is a prominent theme in Christ's teaching about His kingdom, as well as for the prophets who preceded him, who spoke soberly and passionately about communal responsibilities as well as individual complicity.[40]

---

39 Wright, "Jesus is Coming—Plant a Tree!"
40 Matthew 21:28-43, 25:14-30; Mark 12:1-17, 41-44; Luke 20:9-25.

[41] To be made in God's image, to be entrusted with the care of his good creation—to which, as Scripture teaches, He intends to return—bestows enormous responsibilities along with status. It is worth asking how well we're living up to them.

No and Yes

Having made this preliminary effort to sift through a very complex situation, what ought we conclude? To the criticisms made by White and others who followed his lead, we must answer *No*: No, the teaching of the Church is not now, nor has it ever been, consistent with anthropocentric domination or exploitation of the natural world. On the contrary, the consensus of orthodox Christian theology provides strong moral motivation for environmental activism in the highest degree. To their implicit criticisms regarding the overall trend of human behavior in heavily Christianized societies medieval, modern, and today, we must honestly confess *Yes*: Yes, we have at particular times and places failed to follow our own doctrine with rectitude, and thus to communicate it coherently. As a result, some influential individuals as well as groups have made destructive and counterproductive contributions to conservation efforts, through both omission and commission. Our lived belief is not what it should be.

In all, syncretism has been the mutual foe of Christianity and environmentalism alike. The twisting, blending, or suppression of carefully selected theologies so that they either support (or at least do not necessarily oppose) Baconian visions of harnessing nature to for human profit; exploitative private capitalism; short-term gratification to generate wealth; conservative political ideologies; prioritization of correct thinking over obedient discipleship; exclusive relegation of scientific insight to believers who accept as *a priori* and beyond scrutiny certain interpretations of scripture; tenacious Gnostic and Neo-Platonic philosophies

---

[41] Matthew 5-7.

regarding the evils and inadequacies of the natural world and its inevitable and inconsequential destruction; and the disintegration of humanity's dominion commission from its greater biblical context—each tells anew the same tired story of Christianity imperfectly applied to the lived belief of its confessors.

We conclude, then, that syncretism—not Christianity—is environmentalism's true adversary. And we call upon believers of every tradition to re-examine and reaffirm their commitment to God, good creator of a good world, who gave himself to renew the life of that world; who ennobles us, enables us, and commissions us to imitate him, and to participate with him, in realizing "his kingdom come, his will done" on earth as perfectly as it is in heaven.

A version of this paper was previously presented at the 2018 Baylor Symposium on Faith and Culture.

Funeral for a World

Annie Crawford

When someone dies,
the family gathers
beside the still body.
Around a table
they draw near each
other, singing familiar songs
and shared memories—
the moments that mattered,
the words and actions
that revealed the divine soul.

What are we to do
when a world dies?
Where do we gather
when the dead body is ours?
Enemies do not eat
together; they see not the
Other. They shout different songs,
construct different memories—
the moments that matter,
the words and actions,
that reveal our ruined soul.

The center did not hold.
So where will we gather
For the funeral of a world?

    The philosopher Elizabeth Anscombe observed that "what can't be otherwise we accept... but possibility destroys mere acceptance."[1] At the dawn of modernity, the Scientific Revolution expanded the horizon of human possibility, and this awakening of possibility destroyed acceptance. The beginning of rapid technological advancement seemed to imply that man need no longer accept the limitations of the created world. New modes of transportation, communication, production, and medicine made it seemed possible to overcome the limitations of space, time, and perhaps even death. The scientific revolution and its attendant technological progress radically altered the way Western Europeans experienced and thought about the world. While medieval culture had viewed the world as originating from a transcendent, spiritual reality which defined and enlivened the material realm from the inside out, moderns began to view the world as something which could be known and dominated from the outside in. For the ancient and the medieval mind, the fundamental source of being was found in the transcendent realm which was accessed through the inner life of man. For the modern, the externalized material realm became the fundamental locus of being and the spiritual realm was rendered secondary, illusory, or strangely independent. For the past five hundred years, this radical shift has been slowly changing every aspect of Western culture, and here at the dawn of the third millennium, modernism had turned the entire cosmos upside down and inside out.

    The modern shift from a transcendent to a materialist metaphysic transformed what God created to be an expression of his glory into an arbitrary and meaningless collection of dust. The material world has become something to use rather than something to contemplate, and so economic production has now replaced worship as the life-giving center of Western culture. The rationalist endeavor to make human reason the foundation of truth has ironically, as Malcolm Guite explains

---

1 Elizabeth Anscombe, "Contraception and Chastity" (1972), *OrthodoxyToday.org*, accessed February 1, 2018, http://www.orthodoxytoday.org/articles/AnscombeChastity.php.

in *Faith, Hope, and Poetry*, "made for a universe devoid of mind and intrinsically unintelligible."[2] Cut off from a Divine Mind, the reduction of the human mind to a mere material reality has "made mind itself almost an absurdity."[3] No longer sure what it means to be a human, Western culture has regressed into a neo-pagan morality where sexual ethics and the sanctity of life are questioned and even denied. Materialist reductionism has undermined the sacrament of marriage and reduced the meaning of sex to a mere exchange of chemical pleasure (pornography making even physical connection optional). No longer sure what it means to be a human, we mutilate ourselves with surgeries and drugs. Our inability to perceive the transcendental qualities of goodness, truth, and beauty as inherent in the physical world has rendered our society increasingly immoral, incoherent, and ugly.

So here we are, at the end of our world. The old glories are over. At this postmodern juncture, there is nothing left to deconstruct, reduce, or devour. How shall we mourn, we who ourselves are dead? But therein lies our hope, for in a Christ-centered cosmos, death leads to new life. Here at the end of the modern overthrow, we still find ourselves stunned by the mystery of existence. We have doubted everything and now we find ourselves doubting our doubt. We have deconstructed all meaning and yet still find ourselves meaning something. We keep writing poetry. We keep getting married. We still have children, and every newborn child is the renewal of the world.

The meaning we still seek is still present in the world all around us. The heavens have not ceased to declare the glory of God. Day by day, they pour forth speech. Morning, still, "at the brown brink eastward, springs—for the Holy Ghost over the bent world still broods with warm breast and bright wings.[4]

---

[2] Malcolm Guite, Faith, Hope, and Poetry: Theology and the Poetic Imagination (London: Routledge, 2016), 168.
[3] Ibid.
[4] Gerard Manley Hopkins, "God's Grandeur."

The whole of creation, all the "outward 'objects' of nature, they are continuously given and made by the Divine Mind; they are the 'eternal language' of the Divine Poet."[5] The world still speaks. And we still wonder. God has written the truth of his Word into nature and even into our very bodies; if we can learn to again listen to the music of the spheres, to the meaning of the trees, to the meaning of skies and seas, we will rediscover the God who is still there. He will mourn for us, and by the power of His resurrected life renew the world once again.

---

5 Guite, Faith, Hope, and Poetry, 161.

Resources

An Unexpected Journal is published triannually; however, our conversation does not end. Join us online for discussion with the authors weekly:

Online: http://anunexpectedjournal.com
Facebook: https://www.facebook.com/anunexpectedjournal

Comments and feedback can be submitted at http://anunexpectedjournal.com/contact

Read More

When discussing theology, or philosophy, or literature, or art, one is stepping into and taking part of a larger conversation that has been taking place for centuries. Each essay within the journal contains not only the thoughts of the individual author, but draws upon works and thinkers of the past. It is our hope that the writing here not only engages your interest in the specific essay topic, but that you join us in the Great Conversation by looking up the works referenced throughout this *Journal*, reading them for yourself, and sharing your thoughts with others.

Subscribe

Annual subscriptions to *An Unexpected Journal* are available through our website. For more information, please visit http://anunexpectedjournal.com/subscribe.

For bulk pricing, events, or speaking requests, please send an email to anunexpectedjournal@gmail.com.

About An Unexpected Journal

The Inspiration

J.R.R. Tolkien and C.S. Lewis, both members of The Inklings writers group, are well-known for their fiction embedded with Christian themes. These fantasy writers, who were also philosophers and teachers, understood the important role imagination plays in both exercising and expanding the faculties of the mind as well as the development of faith.

Beyond the parables of Jesus, their works are the gold standard for imaginative apologetics. The title, *An Unexpected Journal*, is a nod to the work to which Tolkien devoted much of his life, *The Lord of the Rings*.

Our Story

An Unexpected Journal is the endeavor of a merry band of Houston Christian University Master of Arts in Apologetics students and alumni. What began as simply a Facebook post on November 1, 2017 wishing that there was an outlet for imaginative apologetics quickly organized by the end of the year into a very real and very exciting quarterly publication.

Our Mission

An Unexpected Journal seeks to demonstrate the truth of Christianity, through both reason and imagination, by engaging with culture from a Christian worldview.

Our Contributors

Jasmin Biggs
pilgrimscampfire.substack.com

Jasmin Biggs is a writer, editor, and apologist with a Master of Arts in Cultural Apologetics from Houston Christian University. She is the Editor in Chief at *An Unexpected Journal*; she is also a Bluestocking In Residence with the Society for Women of Letters. She enjoys reading and writing in her local independent bookstore over a cup of espresso. More of her writing may be found at her personal Substack, *A Pilgrim's Campfire*: pilgrimscampfire.substack.com.

Suzanne Carol
https://suzannebroadhurst741768961.wordpress.com/

Suzanne Carol pours forth creative efforts like water from a kettle, often thinking in pictures unveiled as words. She records poetry and prose at Librivox.com; conveys mental health and lifestyle concepts via the arts; and crochets for charities.

Annie Crawford
www.anniecrawford.net

Annie Crawford is a cultural apologist, classical educator, and homeschooling mom whose passion is to help others look at the world around them and see that all truth is God's truth.

For the last two decades, Annie has worked to reintegrate education and discipleship by creating classes, discussion groups, and lectures for both school and church contexts.

In 2014, Annie co-founded Vine Classical Community where she currently teaches apologetics and humanities courses for their Manna program. From 2016-2021, Annie helped develop the Faith & Culture ministry at Christ Church Anglican of Austin, and in 2021 she co-founded The Society for Women of Letters, where she currently serves as Senior

Fellow. Annie also writes for *Salvo, The Symbolic World*, *The Shadowlands Dispatch*, and *An Unexpected Journal*, which she helped found in 2017. Her writing and speaking is focused on the three important "S's" in modern culture: story, sex, and science.

Karise Gililland

Karise Gililland has a BA in English from Southern Methodist University and a Masters in Imaginative and Cultural Apologetics from Houston Baptist University. She consumes copious amounts of time (and coffee!) shuttling her teenagers to and fro, rescuing her cats from impending peril, and writing for An Unexpected Journal. She currently teaches the most amazing third graders at a classical Christian school in Fort Worth.

Sarah Hadley

Sarah Hadley is a graduate student at the University of St Thomas-Houston and a homeschooling mom of four. She has given presentations at the annual ACCS conference and loves encouraging learning within the classical tradition.

Seth Myers

www.narnianfrodo.com

Seth Myers completed his MA in Cultural Apologetics from Houston Baptist University in 2017. As a power systems engineer, he has been involved with transformer diagnostics and rural electrification projects by partnering with NGOs in West Africa. A volunteer with international students through local churches, he enjoys conversations with friends from all cultures. He considers himself rich in friendships across time and space, including but not limited to C.S. Lewis, J.R.R. Tolkien, Bede the Venerable, Augustine, Ravi Zacharias & friends, and many student friends (chess-playing when possible, but not required) typically from throughout Asia. He has recently begun taking online courses in Faulkner University's Doctor of Humanities program.

Annie Nardone

www.AnnieNardone.com

Annie Nardone is an author, educator, and bibliophile who holds an M.A. in Cultural Apologetics from Houston Christian University and is a Fellow with C.S. Lewis Institute. Her writing can be found in *An Unexpected Journal* and the online magazine *Cultivating*. Annie collaborated on three books in 2022, published by Square Halo Books and Rabbit Room. She researched and wrote an historical cookbook for *The Mystery of History-Volume II*. She was on the Founder's Council for The Society for Women of Letters. Annie is writing a curriculum detailing the intersection of the arts and history and is a Master Teacher for HSLDA. Interests include medieval literature, poetry, collecting antiquarian books, and the writings of Lewis and Tolkien.

Josiah Peterson

Josiah Peterson teaches Humane Letters at Chandler Preparatory Academy. He earned his MA in Apologetics from Houston Christian University where he wrote his thesis on C.S. Lewis's rhetoric under the advisement of Holly Ordway and Michael Ward. He lives in Mesa, Arizona with his wife and three children.

Thomas Sims

www.instagram.com/tmsims.poetry/

Thomas Sims holds a B.S. in Biology from the Templeton Honors College at Eastern University. He currently teaches sixth grade science and eleventh grade philosophy/literature in Chandler, Arizona. His work has been featured in *Beyond Words* and *An Unexpected Journal*.

Jason M. Smith

Jason M. Smith is a graduate of the College of William & Mary and of the Cultural Apologetics M.A. program at Houston Christian University. An avid gardener since early childhood, Smith first became interested in Christian conservationism after reading *The Lord of the Rings* during primary school, and has been active in the field ever since.

Smith formerly operated a residential landscape design & installation company specializing in native plants and low-resource gardens. In 1999 he was certified by the National Wildlife Federation as a Steward of suburban wildlife habitat in backyards, small business landscapes, and communities, and subsequently served two years as a Grounds Committee consultant for the township of South Riding, Virginia. He can be reached at jasonmichaelsmith@ymail.com.

Megan M. Starr

Megan M. Starr, M.Ed., M.A. is a C.S. Lewis Institute Fellow who resides in a small town in northeast Ohio where she writes, works as a reference librarian, and hosts a monthly Inklings book club. She is in her twenty-first year of homeschooling and has tutored and taught in classical Christian education settings. She holds an M.A. in Cultural Apologetics from Houston Christian University and is a D.Min. candidate at Houston Theological Seminary, studying faith and culture through the context of death, grief and lament. She also serves as a biblical counselor in her local church. As an avid sports fan, she can usually be found at a ball game, roller skating, or at home, surrounded by any selection of her seven children, 14 chickens, or many books, but not too far from the beeping microwave, where no doubt, she has warmed up her tea for the 10th time.

James M. Swayze
www.adcaelos.com

An apologist and writer, as well as a father of four, Jim lives in Dallas, Texas with his wife, Cristi, two golden retrievers, and two formerly-feral cats. He read Philosophy and English as an undergrad at SMU and obtained a graduate degree in Apologetics from Houston Baptist University. A frequent blogger, Jim travels the United States giving lectures on all things related to C.S. Lewis. For the past few years he has led a popular reading and discussion group called "The Inklings." In his spare time, he likes to fly fish and drink Oregon Pinot noir (though not at the same time).

Joshua Jo Wah Yen
www.joshuajwyen.com

Joshua Yen is an Undergraduate at The University of Oxford reading Philosophy and Theology. He regularly uploads videos on his YouTube and Podcast (Philosophy for All). He has a mission for making education accessible to all both through his social platforms and his university admission program, Logos Education. His works can be found on his website www.joshuajwyen.com and can be contacted at: joshuajwyen@gmail.com.

Thoughts from a Fellow Traveler

By Jack Tollers

If you aren't a Christian and have somehow gotten to the point where you are reading this, then I must warn you about the pebble in your shoe. For that is what it is like to be around Christians who discuss things together, whether or not they are "Christian kinds of things" that are discussed. At a certain point you will notice something about their point of view, something in their underlying assumptions, and to be honest when you do it will become quite annoying.

That is the pebble I was referring to.

But it gets worse.

Maybe it is not your fault that you happen to be reading this, and you've done a pretty good job milling about life without bumping into too much of this sort of Christian stuff. It could be the case that you haven't really made a conscious effort to avoid Christianity, but chances are (if you are reading this) that is going to change. Somewhere along the line, perhaps even in the course of reading this journal, even, a pebble has worked its way into your shoe, and eventually the pebble will have to be dealt with.

It's not my job to tell you what it is. (I don't really know what "it" is in your case. All I know is that when the pebble got into my shoe, it got to the point where I couldn't walk much further without annoying my heel something terrible.) What I can do is suggest to you something that would have helped me if I had come across it in the back of some obscure journal: The pebble does not exist for itself. The pebble makes you stop and deal with the pebble. Stopping to deal with the pebble leads to thinking about your shoe. Then you start thinking about how much further up the trail you'd be if it weren't for that blasted pebble, which leads to thoughts about the trail itself and the path you're walking... and so on.

A particular Christian, or a particular thought expressed by a Christian, or perhaps just the particular quality you meet in places and things of Christian origin will eventually function to put you in mind of something beyond or behind themselves. I say something because I'm trying to be non-partisan, but really I mean someone. Because at some point, the context for these thoughts will change to an awareness that this Christ person has been behind all of it.

When this moment comes, avoid mistaking Jesus for the pebble in your shoe. (If you do, it won't be long before another pebble gets in there and starts the whole thing off again. It took me years to figure that out.) Instead, consider the possibility that he is more like the path than the pebble. He said as much himself when he told Thomas, "I am the way, the truth and the life. No man comes to the Father except by me."

The truth aspect of Jesus' claim is, of course, exclusive. But there is more to his self disclosure. The other terms, "the way" and "the life" point us beyond a mere static assertion of fact or a single point of view toward a dynamic process of relational involvement. The pursuit of truth leads to knowing Jesus (if he indeed is truth incarnate). Thus, just as travelers come to know a country by living in it and exploring it, so people will grow in their knowledge of Truth as they make their way through life, the path itself bringing us in proximity to Jesus.

Such a journey, so conceived, is bound to take a person through some interesting experiences, and to unexpected places. Once the pebble is out of the shoe.

> All the way to heaven is heaven for he said, "I am the way."
> —St. Catherine of Sienna

> "And ye shall seek me, and find me, when ye shall search for me with all your heart."
> —Jeremiah 29:13

PAST ISSUES

If you enjoy discussing faith, apologetics, and culture, don't miss an issue of *An Unexpected Journal*. Find this issues at your online bookstores, digital book sellers, or request your library to carry the journal.

For bulk, corporate, or ministry orders, please contact the journal at anunexpectedjournal@gmail.com

Annual subscriptions may be purchased at http://anunexpectedjournal.com/subscribe

Volume 1 (2018)

Spring: The Abolition of Man

Summer: The Power of Story

Fall: Courage, Strength & Hope

Advent: Planet Narnia

Volume 2 (2019)

Spring: Imagination

Summer: Film & Music

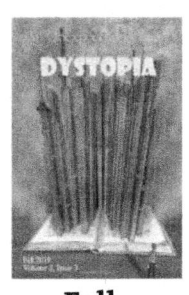

Fall: Dystopia

Advent: G.K. Chesterton

Volume 3 (2020)

Spring: The Worlds of Tolkien

Summer: Science Fiction

Fall: Medieval Minds

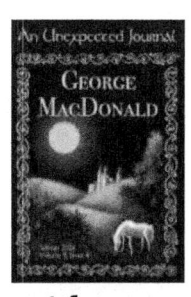

Advent: George MacDonald

Volume 4 (2021)

Spring: Image Bearers

Summer: Super Heroes

Fall: The Ancients

Advent: Ordway's Imaginative Harvest

Volume 5 (2022)

Spring: Saints & Sanctuaries

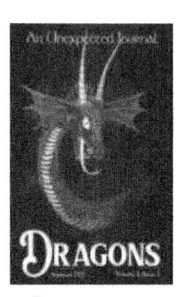

Summer: Dragons

Fall: Joy

Advent: Shakespeare

Volume 6 (2023)

Spring: Mystery

Summer: King Arthur

Fall: Leisure

Advent: Dostoevsky

Volume 7 (2024)

Spring: Modernity

Fall: Community

Advent: Dorothy Sayers

Printed in Great Britain
by Amazon